Nice One Skip

PETER McCONNELL

… WITH ANDY HALL

PRiNT
GRAPHIC
L I M I T E D

First published in 2008 by Andy Hall

Printed in UK by Print Graphic Ltd in 2008

This edition published in 2008

Front Cover main image – Peter McConnell throws his shirt to the crowd at Brunton
Park, 20 April 1965 © Andy Hall
Front Cover inset – Peter with Don Revie, Billy Bremner, Tommy Younger, Freddie
Goodwin, Willie Bell and Derek Mayers at Elland Road © Andy Hall
Back Cover main image – Billy Bremner with the FA Cup at The Angel © Andy Hall
Back Cover inset – Peter doing the half time draw at Brunton Park, Carlisle v Leeds,
20 September 2008 © Barbara Abbott

A CIP catalogue record is available for this book from the
British Library

Printed and bound in the UK by Print Graphic Ltd
Head Office / Design Studio
Warwick Road, Carlisle, Cumbria CA1 1LH
t: 01228 593900 e: info@printgraphic.co.uk
w: www.printgraphic.co.uk

ISBN - 978-0-9560802-0-2

To my mum, who sacrificed so much so that I could follow my dreams, and who followed every kick of the ball with me.

To my wife, Mary, my children Debra, Cath and James, and my wonderful grand-children ... without them there would have been no point.

To my brother Barry – thank you also for your sacrifices.

About the Author

Andy Hall has been Media Officer for Carlisle United Football Club since October 2004, having helped out with the Official Website and the Match Programme at Brunton Park for some two years prior to taking on the role full time.

Also a serving soldier in the Royal Engineers, he completes 24 years of service in May 2009, and was awarded an MBE in 2005 for meritorious service in Afghanistan, Iraq and Northern Ireland.

A keen writer, he is a freelance journalist who covers football match reports and articles for the Sunday Post, Sunday Sun and The Journal, and has a number of titles either already in print, or ongoing.

They include Carlisle United On This Day: History, Facts and Figures from every day of the year (published in October 2008 by Pitch Publishing); Carlisle United Miscellany (published by Pitch Publishing in September 2009) and Each Game As It Comes – Paul Simpson Biography (published by Print Graphic Ltd in 2008 / 2009).

Acknowledgements

Thanks go to Print Graphic Ltd for the work they have done on the layout and design of this book, and their patience as the project unfolded.

Carlisle City Library / Archives deserve a massive mention, for allowing the cross checking of facts and dates contained within the book, and the Cumberland Newspaper Group have been unwitting conspirators, mainly thanks to the scrapbooks and clippings that have been kept together by the McConnell family.

The biggest thanks of all go to Peter, Mary, Debra, Cath and James, and all of those close to them, for allowing me to have a peek behind the scenes at their lives.

From the moment Peter said 'Yeah, why not,' when asked whether he would like to get his stories in to print, to the completion of the book, it has been a hugely enjoyable and uplifting experience – hopefully for us all.

I have found myself taken aback on many occasions as Peter described his escapades involving legends, and I mean true legends, with people like Jack Charlton, Don Revie, John Charles and Billy Bremner, and there have been ear to ear grins as he recounted tales of Carlisle heroes such as Hugh McIlmoyle, Frank Large and 'The Gnomes' (read on – much more on them later!)

Hopefully there will be something in this book for football fans young and old … in fact, I'm confident there will be.

Thanks to you all,

Andy Hall – September 2008

Foreword by George McVitie

I first met Peter McConnell when I was still a schoolboy. I used to go along to Brunton Park to train with the first team on a Tuesday and Thursday evening, and I can honestly say that it was a fantastic experience for me, but it was made even better because of the characters that were in the team at the time.

Peter was the club captain, and he was a man that you couldn't help but like and respect. The thing that stood out for me about him straight away was how professional he was. He always led by example with everything that we did, and he was an extremely hard worker, both on and off the pitch. I remember him being as straight as they come. Nothing was ever hidden with him. If something had to be said, then it was said, but he always made sure that was the end of it. There were never any grudges held, and he was respected by everyone because of the way that he dealt with the people around him. He was one of those men who knew when to shout, when to encourage and when to reason, and he was the focal point for much of what the squad wanted to do or say.

During my early years we would sometimes partner each other during the training sessions for various activities, but I always kept my distance, simply because he was our first team captain and I felt that I had to earn his respect. He was a figure that I looked up, there is no doubt about that, but that became even more the case when I lost my dad when I was just 19 years old. That hit me hard, and there were often times when I felt very down, and I think Peter recognised that. He took me under his wing, really looked after me, and he made sure that I was kept busy if it looked like I might be starting to think about things again. I can remember him telling me that I had to make sure that I looked after my mam, because she would also be feeling very lonely and sad, and that was probably the best bit of advice that I got during what was a very difficult period. It made me realise that I had other responsibilities, and it gave me something to focus on when I was away from the football.

I quickly became Peter's babysitter and, despite the age gap, we became very good friends once I made it in to the squad and started travelling with the team. It was then that I saw first hand the camaraderie within the team … and I also found my way in to the card school that kept us busy on many a long away trip.

On a personal level, it has been a pleasure to have known and worked with Peter. His humour has kept us going more times than I care to remember, and he is always a welcome visitor when he comes back across to Carlisle. As far as the football goes, the influence that he had on what was a fantastic period for the club should not be underestimated. His leadership and guidance helped to steer the club to the upper reaches of Division 2, and it was done through dedication and a belief in excellence in everything that we did. The driving force behind that was Peter McConnell.

I hope you enjoy this book, I know I will, as we look back at the career of a man who is deservedly still spoken about as Carlisle United's longest serving and most influential team captain. As far as descriptions go, that one is as accurate as they come.

George McVitie

Where it all began

I was born on March 3rd 1937 and lived in a moderately sized house on Margaret Street, in Reddish, on the outskirts of Stockport.

My mam was a hard worker, as they all seemed to be back in those days, and she somehow managed to fit in two jobs to help us to make ends meet. She worked in a cotton mill during the day and at night she would put in a shift at the local fish and chip shop. When the mills all started to close down, she went on to work at McVitie's biscuit factory, so she was never shy of doing her bit.

My dad worked in a steel factory in Manchester, and I remember him best as a big, strong bull of a man. His upper arms and forearms were bulging with muscles, so he also found work as a bouncer around some of the pubs and clubs in the City centre. He was such a big man that he could usually talk people out of throwing a punch, even if it was just by glaring at them. If he was on nights, he would also go on a coal delivery round to help his friend out during the afternoons, so I grew up knowing that the only way to get anything out of life was to work for it. I don't think that was too bad an outlook to have, all things considered.

He was a good footballer, a strong centre half, but he had a nasty temper whenever he went out on to the pitch. He was sent off almost every week when he played for Droylsden, and there was one memorable occasion when my mother was hitting the spectators stood around her with her handbag as he made his way for an early bath, just because they were booing him as he walked off. She'd put up with most things, but she wasn't about to see her man getting that kind of treatment. During the war years he actually guested for Manchester City, and that was something that he was extremely proud of.

His first name used to cause some amount of consternation during games, especially when the Referee would call him over and ask him for it, so that he could be booked for his latest indiscretion. Dad would quite rightly say, 'I'm Clarence McConnell.' More often than not the Ref would look at him and tell him that if he didn't stop messing about he'd be getting his red card out, so dad would sigh and say, 'Alright, call me Charlie McConnell then, it makes no difference to me.'

My younger years were spent listening to the grown-ups talking about the war, mixed in with the excitement of running to the shelters during the air raids, whilst we then gathered around the radio to get the latest news on what was happening on Mainland Europe.

I can remember overhearing people saying that the big football ground, over at Old Trafford, had been struck during one particular air raid. I was too young, at the time, to fully appreciate what the bombing raids really meant to us all but, having since seen pictures of the damage that was done in the area, and around the rest of the country, I do often wonder how we managed to get through it all in such high spirits. All of the parents, especially the mums, seemed to do their best to make sure that life went on as normally as possible and, as daft as it may sound, it was a very happy time for us children.

We actually had an air raid shelter in our back yard, which we all used to run to when the sirens went off, but it could sometimes be a complete waste of time. With my dad being a steel worker, he wasn't sent away to fight, as he was needed to make the bits and pieces for the tanks and ships, and for the other stuff that was being used by the forces. This meant that he also kept up with his afternoon coal round. At the end of each shift him and his mate would bring spare coal back to the house, and dump it in our shelter, making it damn near impossible for us to get in when we needed to. My mother never used to say anything about it to him though, because I think she was just happy to have the coal.

When I went round to visit my grandmother, air raids were always a bit of an adventure. She didn't have a shelter in her back yard, so we used to huddle together under the table, in the back room of her Haberdashery shop, and wait for it to be over. Looking back it seems a stupid thing to have done, but we knew no different, and we must have had lady luck on our side because we all lived to tell the tale.

By the time I was eight years old the war was over and things really did start to get back to normal. That meant school and football … or maybe that should be football and school in my case. We didn't have any playing fields, as such, so all of our games were played out on the streets. That was a real test in itself, because not only were they fairly narrow and uneven, but they were cobbled, often with huge gaps between the stones. We used our jackets as goal posts and that was the source of many an argument, I can tell you. There was one occasion when I think we spent more time arguing over whether a goal had been scored, than we did actually playing the game, so you needed a strong character as well as a strong tackle to make sure that you were League champions by the time it got dark.

Sometimes we were allowed to play on in to the night, under the gaslight, and I think they were some of the happiest days I can remember from my childhood. There were no distractions at all – no TV, no computers, no mobile phones, just a bunch of kids and whichever competition we could come up with to pass away a few hours each evening. I think the only real piece of technology that we had on our street was a big, red phone box that stood on the corner. As far as we were concerned though, that was just another goal post, until we got told off and it was back to the jackets and the arguments.

Shortly before my brother Barry came along, not long after the war, my father almost achieved what the Germans hadn't managed. He'd had a long shift and had gone straight to bed, so he had no idea that our next door neighbours had sprung a gas leak. When he woke up he shouted for my mother, but she was otherwise engaged outside on the toilet.

My dad was a man of routine, and he always had a woodbine when he first got downstairs, so he went in to the kitchen to light it. As soon as he struck the match the house next door exploded in a ball of flames. My poor mum came running out of the toilet, with her underwear round her ankles, screaming, 'WHAT HAVE YOU DONE, WHAT HAVE YOU DONE' and all he did was shake his head and moan on that nobody had warned him that there was a gas problem in the house next door.

Game On

At weekends we all used to go down to a place called Houldsworth Square, in Stockport, where we would jump on to the Melba Coaches and head off towards Maine Road. It was a win-win situation for everyone at the time, because both City and United shared the ground, due to the bomb damage at Old Trafford, so there was a game for us to watch on our doorstep almost every single week.

It's probably fair to say that I was a Manchester United fan, because they had some wonderful players and played some fantastic football. My fascination with them was partly because they won the FA Cup in 1948, but mostly because three of their players, John Carey, Jack Rowley and Henry Cockburn, came to visit us at North Reddish Primary school, and I was completely star struck by them. I was only eleven at the time, and they were like Gods, real heroes to me, and I hung on to every word they said.

To this day I can still recite the starting line up of that United team and I think, at one point or other during those games on our cobbled streets, I've imagined being each and every one of them:

Crompton

Carey   Aston

Anderson   Chilton   Cockburn

Delaney   Morris   Rowley   Pearson

Mitten

What a team! Charlie Mitten had a great left foot, and he was also their penalty taker. He went on to make headlines, along with the Stoke City centre half Neil Franklin, when the pair of them flew off to play for Bogota. Players jetting off to play abroad were unheard of back then, and their decision caused quite a stir for a number of weeks. John Carey was another wonderful player, as was Cockburn, and the strength they had in depth was breathtaking. It was a pleasure to have been able to watch them.

That year was also my dreaded 11+ year, but I surprised myself by doing quite well, despite having spent most of my revision time by practicing my step over and keep-ups in the back yard. That must have driven our neighbours to distraction, but none of them ever said anything or they'd have had my mother to deal with. She was a fierce competitor, especially where her family was involved, and there was only ever one winner in arguments like that.

She was football crazy as well and I'm sure that, if she'd been born a boy, she'd have played the game as much as I did. Although we were never well off, she always made sure that I had a new pair of football boots and a new lace-up leather football at Christmas, and that is something that I will always thank her for.

I moved on to the Milend Secondary School, in Stockport, and quickly got myself a place in their football team. If I'm being honest, they were never really renowned for the standard of team they put out, but it was football, and that was all that mattered to me. I used to play for them on a Saturday morning, and then I'd quickly sort myself out in readiness for a game with my local team on the Saturday afternoon. Sometimes, if I was lucky, they wouldn't be playing until the Sunday … mind you, I'd still find a game to be involved in on the afternoon anyway, so I don't suppose it really made that much of a difference at all.

The manager of the Saturday afternoon team was a man called Frank Aspinall. He was a local character, who had a real love for the game, and I think he had three teams on the go at one point, just so he could involve as many good, young players as possible. He would often be seen riding round the area on his bike, looking out for players that he thought he could use in his teams. He was very complimentary of the way that I liked to play, and he pretty much allowed me to do what I wanted once I got out on the pitch, and that was something that I obviously enjoyed.

All things told, it was quite a competitive area that we lived in, so the Stockport Parks Department organised what they called a Kerbside Cup competition for us. They said it was a good way to keep us off the streets, but it was a football mad area and it was always going to be a success, whatever reasons were given. Frank asked us if we wanted to play in it, and we all said yes almost right away. He decided to call us 'The Brigadoons' (I have no idea why) and, after checking that we really did want to go for it, he registered us that same week.

It was all very exciting, and we treated it as seriously as we could, because we were determined to do well and give a good account of ourselves. It quickly became apparent that we were one of the better teams of the 71 that had entered, and we knew from an early stage that we were in with a real chance of going all the way. Five games later, including two away wins and three victories on our home ground at Houldsworth Park, and we were through to the final. That turned out to be an unbelievable and truly unforgettable experience for us all.

It was played at Edgeley Park, the Stockport County ground, and there were all sorts of important people lined up to watch us. The Lord Mayor of Stockport, Mr Lowe, opened things up, but the real buzz was finding out that Manchester City legend Frank Swift was also going to be there to meet us and wish us luck. He was an absolute giant of a man and, typical for a goalkeeper, he had hands like JCB buckets. A full England international, as well as the City number one, he tragically died in the Munich Air Disaster of 1958 when he travelled out to follow Manchester United in his capacity as a football reporter.

The final itself was my first real taste of success. We won a hard fought game by 2-1 against Bredbury United, in front of a crowd of 5000 which, incidentally, was 1500 more than had watched the Saturday game between Stockport County and Rotherham. It was a very proud day for our family, because my younger brother Barry was our mascot. To top it all off, I had a hand in both of the goals, from my inside right position, and that gave us all something to smile about at full time. The newspaper gave the event some really good coverage, calling it a miniature Wembley, and the report said – Brigadoon's right half back, the 13-year-old Peter McConnell, son of Clarence McConnell the former Droylsden professional, was a little magician with the ball. Well, I can't remember being a magician, but I do know that I had a very enjoyable day.

We celebrated in the changing room afterwards with water, splashing it over each other as if it was champagne and Frank took us for a potato pie supper, which was a wonderful treat, before we all headed off home to our dreams of future glory.

I felt in myself that I had played well, and I must have made the right kind of impression because not long afterwards I was invited along to trial for the Stockport Boys. They also played at Edgeley Park, and the standard of football that they produced was a real step up. The trial went well, really well in fact, and I was invited along to join the team for their training sessions ahead of their next run of games.

I was almost 14 years old by now, and I found that I was enjoying myself, playing with lads who could really use the ball, with the added bonus that my own game was improving all the time. I was becoming fitter and stronger, and I didn't feel out of place in any way. Again, the coaches were more than happy with my progress, and I was brimming with confidence, so it was just a case of waiting to see where it would lead – if indeed it was going to go anywhere.

Decision Time

Eventually, when I was 15, I was selected to play for the Cheshire Boys team and football became the only thing that I wanted to do. I'd always dreamed that I would go on to play for one of the big teams, like many young boys do, but it goes without saying that there are never any guarantees in football. I'd worked hard, and I'd trained hard, but you do have those nights when you wonder if it will happen for you. To get the call up to the County team gave me a real boost, and I decided there and then that I was going to give it everything I had.

They played me in the inside right position, wearing the number 8 shirt, and it was a role that I took to with ease. I earned myself a place in the starting line up, and my confidence grew with every ball that I kicked. I'd heard a few whispers that scouts were coming out to watch the games, but it was simply a case of putting that to the back of my mind and getting out there to do my job. I knew that if I played to the best of my ability, then I would be giving them something to think about, and I kept hoping that was going to be enough.

Ultimately, it was, because five of us were called together after the second game that we played, against Lancashire Boys, and we were told that we had an invitation to go along to Elland Road to attend some trials. It was explained to us that we were going to be given a month to show the staff over there what we could do, so we had to make sure that it was something that we were really going to give our best efforts to. It's difficult to describe the emotions that I felt when I heard that news – excitement, pride, anxiety, joy – probably a bit of all of them, but what I did know was that there was no way that I was going to mess it up. I'd hoped and prayed for a chance, and I knew full well that another one might not come along, so I was going to grab this one with both hands.

My parents weren't able to come with me to the trials, but one of the lads that I went across to Leeds with was called Billy Flitcroft. It was a new experience for us, travelling by train and tram, but we worked it all out between us. He was from a family of footballers, really good stock, and there were days when he stood out head and shoulders above all of us. I fully expected him to be one of the ones to make it but, after a very testing trial period, I was the only one asked to stay behind by the United coaching staff. Still, to this day, I wonder why Billy never made it. He could do things that the rest of us could only dream about, so I suppose he became a very good example of how sometimes the breaks just don't happen, whatever the reason for that may be.

Having been through the sessions and having listened as intently as I could whenever the coaches had opened their mouths, I found that my heart was racing a bit when it came to my turn to be told whether I'd been successful or not. I'd enjoyed myself, and I hadn't needed to be spoken to on my own, or anything like that, but I had a horrible, unshakeable feeling that I hadn't quite done enough. Don't get me wrong, I knew that I'd done alright, but there were moments in each of the trial periods where I felt that I could and should have done better, and that was niggling away in the back of my mind.

It was a huge relief when they told me that I'd been accepted and I felt like punching the air when they finally confirmed that they wanted me to sign forms with them. Unfortunately, there was still one big stumbling block – my parents had to agree that I could leave school, without doing any GCE exams, and the school also had to agree that they were willing to let me go.

Mum and dad knew exactly how much I wanted to be a professional footballer, and they knew that Leeds were a massive club, so they left the decision up to me. In fact, my mum's whole attitude towards it was – go for it Peter! Academically, I could hold my head above water, but it just wasn't something that I enjoyed. There was nothing worse for me than to be sat at a desk when, just a few feet the other side of the window, there was grass to be played on and a football to be kicked.

The school recognised this and they seemed happy with the situation, when it was explained to them, but they still made their position quite clear to all three of us. Basically, they told me that if I left, and if it didn't work out, then there was no going back. They weren't going to suddenly reopen their gates to me and allow me to sit any of the exams that I'd missed. I was moving on at my own risk ... I suppose they were telling me in a roundabout way that they were washing their hands of me. I weighed that advice up, pondered on it for all of about 30 seconds, threw my eggs in to one basket anyway, and off I went to the bright lights of the big City over in Leeds.

It'll be all white on the night

So, there I was, a young lad with his first attempt at a 'DA' haircut, not long out of short trousers, with a suitcase full of not very much at all, a list of instructions from my mum that seemed to be all about what not to do, and a determination to make it work, however hard things were going to be.

Up to that point, the furthest from home I had ever been was a place called Clevelys, near Blackpool, where we used to go for our annual family holiday. The word daunting doesn't really do that whole situation justice, but I knew that I had to get my head down and just get on with it.

The club put me in to digs at a place called Beeston, not too far from the ground. The landlady was a lovely woman called Mrs Nickelson, and she brought a smile to my face every time I saw her, simply because she looked like Les Dawson when he was doing his drag act.

My weekly wage was the princely sum of £5, and that was pretty much accounted for almost as soon as I got it. £2-50 went to Mrs Nickelson for my board, £1 went straight to my mum, and that left me with £1-50 to spend on myself. Mind you, I still felt like a king, especially when you consider that I was being paid for doing something that I loved.

She put me in her attic, complete with skylight, along with a room mate who turned out to be an extremely eccentric chap called Bob. He was a Scotsman, and he seemed friendly enough, but it was strange to have to share a room with someone that I had only just met.

On my very first night in the house with him, I woke up at about midnight, with the moonlight shining right through the skylight and in to my face. I turned over, towards Bob, and found myself face to face with a glass of water, complete with a false eye bobbing up and down on top of it. Was I scared … you bet your life I was! It took me ages to get back to sleep, and I kept asking myself over and over, as I fretted away - 'What the heck have you got yourself in to here?'

I asked him about it the next morning, and he was fine about it, and we got on really well after that. In a way, he kept me right with a lot of things, and it was good to have some company at the end of each day. Just in case you're wondering, the one-eyed man was not Gary Sprake!

After breakfast on that first morning I made my way along to the ground, where I was introduced to the rest of the new intake. They called us 'Groundstaff Boys' and we quickly found out why. There were eight of us in total, and our first job was to sweep all of the rubbish out of the stands, the terraces and the corridors, and then dump it on to a tip that was just down the road. It always used to make me laugh when people asked about the glamorous lifestyle, because I definitely didn't see any of it in those early days.

In fact, when you see footballers these days they all seem to have at least three really big cars, with a choice of which one to go to work in depending on the kind of mood that they are in that day. They have sports cars, range rovers, top of the range off roaders - you name it, they have it. Mind you, we always had three choices when we were playing as well – we either got the bus, the tram or we walked!

I think there would only have been four, maybe five at a push, of the first team players who owned a car when I first got to Elland Road. It was just something that was almost unheard of. John Charles had one, the captain Tommy Burden had one, and Albert Nightingale got himself one just after I got there. Other than that, they weren't a common sight at all.

I was reading an article in the paper not long ago that was written by a man called Keith Miller. He was an Australian all-rounder who used to amaze the cricket crowds around the time when I first got to Leeds, and he was discussing the fact that modern-day footballers often seem to complain about stress related illnesses. He explained that he was a fighter pilot during World War 2, and there was one afternoon when he was flying his Spitfire back towards his home base. Something didn't feel right, so he'd taken a look over his shoulder and there, almost close enough to touch, was a Messerschmitt glued to his tail. He'd laughed at the attitude of the modern sportsmen and said, '… a Messerschmitt up your backside – now that's what I call stress!'

It turned out that the rest of the Youth lads were also staying in Beeston, at a place called Mrs Humphrey's Ranch House. Although imaginatively named, it was just another Bed and Breakfast, and it meant that I could meet up with them after our days work was over, without having to go too far to do it.

One of the jobs that we all hated as ground staff was rolling the pitch after a game. The club had this roller that was bigger than the entire Youth squad put together. It had two shafts attached to it, and it was clearly meant to be pulled by a Shire horse, or something even more substantial than that, but we ended up with three on each shaft and four on the roller part itself, just to get the damn thing moving. Turning corners must have been a right sight.

To alleviate the monotony we used to regularly hide balls round the back of the stand, so that we could get them out again whilst we were meant to be working. If the head groundsman was out of sight, we'd down tools and have a kick around. We'd take it in turns to be lookout, and as soon as he came back in to view we'd hide the balls again and pretend that we'd been hard at it. Heaven only knows how we didn't get caught.

Obviously we also got to play our football for real, and one of the other lads that looked a bit special was a Welsh boy called John Reynolds. Even at that young age, they were talking about him as the next John Charles. Not only was he a fabulous footballer, but he was also a lovely lad, and there was a general agreement that he was going to go all the way.

One of my clearest memories of him was the pleasure that he took in working with a pitch fork down at the tip. Every time we were on clean up duty he would get himself a fork from the utility hut and become public enemy number one for every rat in sight. I don't think he ever missed.

Sadly, it all went wrong for him in a terrible way. We drew West Brom in the fifth round of the FA Youth Cup, and they were a really good team. Their captain was Don Howe, who later went on to become a very distinguished player with Arsenal and England, and it was a really closely fought game. John was playing well again, and living up to expectations, when he went over on his leg and ended up in a heap on the floor. We later found out that he'd snapped his cruciate ligament, and we knew that there was very little hope of him making a return. Typical of John, he kept his chin up despite the injury, and he made sure that the rest of us kept doing the things that we had to do whilst he went through his rehab process.

Eventually, when it became clear that he wasn't going to recover, he was given a job with the head groundsman, Ces Burrows. When Ces retired, Don Revie had a word with John and offered him the role, and we were all delighted when he accepted it. He genuinely was one of the nice guys, and it was good that things worked out for him in that way.

I found a newspaper clipping recently, written by a Leeds reporter called Phil Brown, who had decided that he was going to cover the game over at the Hawthorns for us. There was quite a bit of interest in how we were playing, and more and more fans had started to come along to watch us, so he took the opportunity to capitalise on that and he did a little pen picture on each of the members of the squad ahead of the kick off. He wrote this about me – The right half is the captain, Peter McConnell, from Stockport, a stocky lad who is growing nicely, and developing his football nicely too. On John he had written – Centre-forward is John Reynolds, from Briton Ferry, South Wales, and likely to be big as he is 5ft 10in and over 11st already. Another tipped to make it was Malcolm Lawton – There is only one Leeds boy in the side, and he is one of the stars. Malcolm Lawton, the right back, a product of Leeds United Colts and a lad who lives near to the Elland

Road ground is strongly built and with courage to match, he is a tackler indeed. We all saw the article that Phil did in the paper, and it was nice to read that other people thought that you were doing the right things as well.

One of the other jobs we had to do on a Monday was clean the first team players' boots, and we had a special boot room where we had to go to do it. We had a young lad called Billy who worked in there, making the studs, and he had it down to a really fine art. It wasn't like these days where you could screw them in and out, because they were all fashioned from leather, either as long or short, depending on the weather. He had pliers to pull the old stud out, and he would sometimes leave bits of it on there, so that all he had to do was make a top to go on it – and that would be job done for another game. Billy was a genius with his tools and he could shape your studs so that nobody could tell they'd been worked on, unless they got really close.

He had a trick for the frosty weather that would have got him hung if the authorities had ever found out. He'd wait until the Referee had inspected the studs in the pre-match build up, and then he'd start to take a couple of layers of the leather off. He'd then tap a false cardboard top on to the nail and, again, you couldn't tell the difference unless you got yourself really close to it.

The players would then make sure that they scuffed their studs as they made their way down the tunnel and out on to the pitch, and by the time they crossed the white line they were running around on leather based studs that had a nail sticking out of the top for extra grip. It used to give our players a huge advantage, and it actually became quite widespread practice. When you see the fourth official asking the player to lift his boot up these days, that goes all the way back to the 1950's and 60's when we used to have these leather and nail studs that teams would fiddle with in any way that they could as they tried to gain that extra little edge.

Mind you, I was a very thoughtful chap, so I used to cover my studs in iodine just in case I cut anyone when I was tackling them. I didn't want it to get infected now did I!

Growing Up

I used to make sure that I kept an eye on everything that was going on around Elland Road and I soon got an idea of how the pecking order worked, and I could see how the management and directors employed different techniques to help to foster competition for places at all levels. For example, at Christmas the directors used to treat the squad with a few birds – of the feathered variety! A list would appear on the wall that looked something like this:

First Team Players – Turkey
Second Team Players – Duck or Goose
Third Team players – Chicken

As ground staff we received an extra £1 in our wage packet for the festive period, so you can see that we were already being made to understand the benefits behind making the grade.

Another lesson that would come slightly later, but it's worth mentioning now, was when it snowed overnight ahead of a big FA Cup game with Derby. Every single available man had a shovel in his hand as soon as he got to the ground and the pitch was cleared and deemed playable about half an hour before kick off. Internationals, players with huge reputations, experienced players and youngsters; they were all side by side making sure that whatever had to be done to get the game on was done. That's another example of the way the club worked – football was everything.

The manager when I first started at Leeds was a man called Major Frank Buckley. He was an old man, in his 70's, and he used to cut a fine dash in his plus fours and deerstalker. He had some weird ways, and he installed some punch bags in the gymnasium area – the type that are strung from the ceiling to the floor and also the conventional, larger type – and he used to demonstrate how fit he was by kicking and punching them both as if he was a teenager.

Things possibly turned in my favour with him when, for one of the first against second team practice matches, I was asked to run the line. I was getting on with that as efficiently as I could when Major Buckley started waving at me. The number 4, a player called Eric Kerfoot, had got himself injured and he looked to be in quite a bad way. Eric had been in the first team for years, and suddenly I was expected to take his place. I never really looked back after that. To be fair to Eric, he also took me under his wing, as he seemed to take a liking to me, and that gave me a real boost of confidence.

Unfortunately, Major Buckley was sacked just a few weeks after that incident. That was a double blow for me, because he'd finally got to know my name after months of struggling to remember me. Almost without fail, prior to replacing Eric, he would see me in the corridor, perhaps doing one of my jobs or carrying some equipment around, and he would ask me who I was and what I was doing. I'd tell him, and he'd nod or tell me to 'get on with it then' only for us to have to go through the same routine the following day. That was frustrating, because you never really knew where you stood with him so, like I say, I was disappointed when I found out that he had gone, and particularly as it was just as he had finally worked out who I was.

I wasn't the only one who had that problem either because we had two very good goalkeepers at the time called Roydon Wood and Jack Scott. They were vying for the number one shirt, but neither of them were filled with confidence when Major Buckley would regularly ask the pair of them which was which … and what position they played.

The fact that I'd played with the first team and the Reserves gave me a real head start within the Leeds Youth set up. They switched me from number 8 (inside right) to number 4 (right half) and it was a move that really suited me. I was captain of the team even though I was still only 16 years old, and we played so well that we did the double and enjoyed a good FA Youth Cup run, with me taking quite a lot of responsibility out on the field.

I had also attended a behind closed doors trial for the selectors of the England U18 Youth team, at Belle Vue in Doncaster, and although I didn't go on to make it in to the team, the reports that were sent back to Elland Road from the day were very complimentary.

The coaches were pleased with my progress, so I ended up playing with the Reserves in the Central League. That was an excellent education for me football wise, and one that I feel stood me in good stead throughout the rest of my career. One of my very good friends from the successful Youth team, Malcolm Lawton, made the step up with me, and we became quite a formidable pair. If they got past me, they then had him to deal with - and they would never get past him twice, let's put it that way.

6

A New Man

Our new manager was an ex-England inside forward called Raich Carter. He was a stern character, some would say perhaps a bit of a bully at times, and there were days when you knew that you had to tread carefully with him.

Raich wasn't very popular with the players at all, if I'm going to be totally honest, because he seemed to struggle when it came to dealing with people on a one-to-one basis. He was a big headed man; one of those who had been there and done it bigger and better than you ever had … or ever could for that matter. He was a good player, there's no argument about that, but he used to try to intimidate people to bring them round to his way of thinking, and that's not something that I have ever had much time for. If you dared to speak out against him, there was hell to pay, and he would then make your life very difficult indeed.

I used to play up against him in our practice matches, and he had a marvellous left boot on him. His quality on the ball used to shine through, but it was his personality that I found difficult to deal with. If, for example, a player was going through a tough time, or if he felt that a player wasn't really good enough, then instead of coaching or encouraging him, he would go the other way. It was almost as if he switched off to the fact that they were even there, because you could either do it or you couldn't in his eyes.

Mind you, most of the managers back then were ex-players with international caps and often with very distinguished careers behind them. That's all very well, but it doesn't always make for someone who will bring you instant success. There's so much more to management than just being able to play the game, and many clubs found that out to their peril with some of the appointments that they made.

As a Youth player, not just at Leeds United, but everywhere, you were expected to work hard and get on with things, whoever the manager was, and you were never really kept abreast of how well you were doing. Having made the Reserves and captained the Youth team, I felt that I was probably doing alright, but there were days and nights when doubt would creep in. I should have known that I was well thought of, though, because on top of the general jobs that we were given, I was also tasked with cleaning the managers' car. I was expected to do that weekly, and it was one of those chores that usually went hand in hand with being a player that the gaffer wanted to have a closer look at.

He summoned me to his office on my 17th birthday and, despite playing the 'what does he want me for, does anyone know' game, I knew exactly what was happening. He had clearly made a decision on whether to offer me a contract or not. I knocked, waited a while and, for a confident lad, I can honestly say that it was the most nervous I have ever been in my life. As I said, I felt that I'd done as much as anyone to deserve a contract, but you just never knew. I suppose the real problem was that there was no Plan B. I hadn't even considered what I would do if I didn't make it in football, and suddenly my very own 'D' Day was upon me. It was going to be a shock for me if he told me to leave, and I have no idea how I would have reacted if that is what had happened on that day.

Anyway, he called me in and, I'm very pleased to say, he wasted no time at all in getting to the point. He said, 'Peter, you will be delighted to know that I want to sign you as a professional.' He looked up at me and I think I just smiled, or something equally as daft. He added, 'I'm going to give you a £20 signing on fee, and you'll get £12 a week during the season and £10 a week during the summer. What do you reckon to that lad?'

I paused, and knowing that he was happy with a bit of banter, said, 'Well, that's not bad, but John Charles (a real Leeds legend, by the way) gets £12 a week during the summer as well, so surely I should be the same Boss?' He gave me one of his withering looks, swore a bit, then smiled at me and said, 'OK lad, if you ever get as good as he is, I'll give you the pay rise. I can't say fairer than that now can I? Now on you go.'

21

7

Lads Army

During my early years at Leeds, always in the background for me was the fact that I knew that I still had the small matter of National Service ahead of me. All fit and able bodied boys of 18 years of age had to do it, and football players were no exception.

After fitting in two friendlies in the first team a few of us, including John Reynolds and myself, headed off to Catterick for our basic training. We were gutted when John was medically discharged after just a few days, because of his knee injury, and I know that he felt really down about it as well. They were tough times for all of us, to be honest, but we were used to discipline and we were in good physical shape anyway, so we were able to cope with that side of things better than most.

Eight weeks after my arrival in Catterick I passed out as a B3 Wireless Operator. I kept myself as fit as I could, because I wasn't really interested in working with radios, and I eventually managed to get myself a transfer in to the Gym, as an instructor.

The club had moved us to new digs in Beeston just before we joined up, and I was living with a lovely old lady called Mary Crowther. Her daughter Laura used to help her run things, and between them they kept us in line and out of trouble.

My room mate this time was a lad called Dilwyn Jones and we couldn't have got on any better than we did. We had an absolutely great time. Whenever we went out we wore club blazers and badges, and we carried a player's pass that used to get us in to the Majestic and Scala cinemas and dance halls. As you can imagine, we made full use of that.

As far as National Service was concerned, that player's pass proved to be worth much more than its weight in gold. Whilst on barracks, we had a leave clerk called John who was put in charge of our weekend and evening passes, and our leave cards. I somehow found out that he'd just got engaged, and that he was struggling a bit on the financial side because all that he had was what the army paid him ... and that wasn't very much at all. As luck would have it, I bumped in to him and his fiancée at the Scala dance hall one Saturday evening, and I offered to let him have my player's pass on weekends, so he could treat his young lady to a decent night out. He was over the moon, as was his girlfriend and, in return, I ended up with a steady procession of weekend and night time passes, and extra leave periods. That meant that I could either go home, or back to my digs in Beeston, and it got me off camp and gave me some breathing space, even if it was just for a short while. The news that I was to be posted to Germany, with still twelve months of my National Service to serve, was bad for us all as it brought an abrupt end to our cosy arrangement.

Germany was a good experience, to be fair, and it was there that I perfected the art of looking busy. The theory behind it is really quite simple. First thing in the morning I would arm myself with a clipboard and a piece of blank paper, and set off on a walk around camp. If anyone saw me, or looked like they were going to ask me what I was doing, I would raise the clipboard up in front of me and start to scribble on it. Once they'd moved on, I'd wander off in the opposite direction. By the time I came to demob I had the procedure down to a tee, and no-one ever seemed to cotton on.

I also thoroughly enjoyed the work in the gymnasium, and used the opportunity it presented to keep myself as fit as I possibly could. Although I was working for the army, my focus was still on becoming a professional footballer with Leeds United once my stint with National Service was done, and everything that I did during those two years was with that in mind. The best way to describe it, I suppose, is that my time with the military got in the way. It wasn't a complete waste of time, as nothing in life ever is, but it definitely wasn't where I wanted to be. I had other things that I needed to be getting on with.

One real positive was that the opportunities for playing football were more frequent with the British Army of the Rhine (BAOR) and I was selected to play for the 1st Armoured Division (Desert Rats) against Rommel's lot. Thinking back, we had an excellent team on show that day, with a few players who had played at professional clubs in our side. Ray Pointer, who was on the books at Burnley and who went on to play for England, was our centre forward and we had others who knew how to use a ball. By half time we were 7-0 up, and I think it's the only time I've ever had a bollocking for playing well. Our camp Colonel came in to the dressing room and tore strips off us, screaming at us about public relations and hearts and minds, and he all but ordered us to ease off and give them a chance in the second half. Thankfully that's the only time I ever heard anything like that throughout my whole career.

On my return from National Service in 1957 we had a demob party, and it was there that I met football's first ever WAG (only kidding Mary). My eye was drawn to her because she was stood off to one side, talking quietly amongst her friends, and I thought she was the double of Liz Taylor.

I did some digging, and I found out that she worked at Mathias Robinson's, a big Department Store in Leeds. I got talking to her, and we got on really well, so we arranged to meet for lunch the following Friday, once I'd finished training. This became a regular date, and things moved on for us rather quickly from there.

From the Draft to the Graft

Raich Carter was eventually sacked as manager, with the Directors looking for better results, and they brought a man called Bill Lambton in to do the job. I have never really understood the thinking behind this decision, other than they seemed to want someone in charge who would instil a bit of discipline. Perhaps Bill did that, but I'm more inclined to think that most of the players switched off to his antics not long after he arrived.

By now I was 20 years old, and I wanted to get my football career back on track at Leeds United. I knuckled down and I soon found myself playing in the Reserve side, and enjoying a small amount of success. I finally got my full League debut just before I turned 21, in a home game against Bolton Wanderers. That one came as a huge surprise to me because I was actually on the bus and ready to head off to play in an away game with the rest of the Reserve team. My name was shouted out, just before we pulled off, and I was told, as I was making my way down the aisle, that I had better get myself ready because I was playing for the first team in what was quite an important game. Me being me, my first thought was that I'd just missed out on my £1 away travel meal voucher, and I was trying to work out if there was any way that I could claim it anyway!

I think the whole situation surrounding my debut probably worked in my favour. It all happened so quickly, from being hauled off the team bus to getting changed in the dressing room, that I didn't have time to dwell on it. It was quite literally a case of getting amongst it and getting on with it in the best way that I could.

The Bolton team back in those days was an extremely strong one. I remember Tommy Banks, their full back, because he had one heck of

25

a reputation as being a very strong character. He was another from the mould that would never let anyone pass and, if they did evade him, it wasn't going to be happening twice. Up front they had the one and only Lion of Vienna himself – Sir Nat Lofthouse. He really looked the part in every way. He was strong in the air, powerfully built and he seemed to have at least a yard on everyone else, in any given situation.

As for the game itself, I can't remember that much about it. I can recall the noise from the crowd, and the excitement of the goals but, as you can probably appreciate, it was such a fantastic day for me that it seemed to fly by. What I do know, and it's a thing that makes me swell with pride even when I think about it today, is that both teams got a standing ovation when the final whistle was blown. Bolton stole it with a 4-3 win, but it was end to end and both sides really went for it. It could have gone either way, but they took their chances, and I think the Leeds fans appreciated the fact that we went toe to toe with one of the best teams in the country, and we matched them man for man. I can remember having a hand in at least one of the goals, and I also recall being determined to do my bit, and I don't think I stopped running at all during the 90 minutes. As far as debut games go, I don't think I could have asked for a better arena or for better opponents. I have many wonderful memories from my time in football and, it probably goes without saying, that this game is right up there with the best of them.

Nat Lofthouse was always the one that the press wanted to speak to in the post-match conferences, because of his stature and standing, and we were all interested to hear who he thought was the best crosser of a football in the game at the time. The two names he fired back, almost straight away, were Tom Finney and Stanley Matthews. There could be little argument about that, and I'm proud to say that I played against both of them later in my career. When he was pushed on which of the two was the better, he politely declined to be drawn, simply stating that they were both as good as each other. However, he qualified that with the comment, 'All I will say is that Stanley always manages to cross the ball so that the laces are facing away from my forehead, which I do appreciate.'

I spent most of the rest of that season in the Reserve side, which was a huge disappointment having been involved in such a big game, but I was brought back in for the Blackpool match at Bloomfield Road as the campaign drew to a close. Concerns were being raised over the erratic form of the otherwise reliable Archie Gibson, and it was decided that I would take his place. That was the start of a very good run of games for me, and it seemed to coincide with an upturn in results as we all but killed off any lingering relegation fears. Having waited so long and worked so hard I could only hope that I'd done enough to carry my selection in to the next season, and I knew that it was going to be an agonising wait through the summer.

The fans took to me initially, I'm pleased to say, because I wasted no time or sympathy when going in for a tackle. There was one occasion, at Newcastle, where I have no idea how a red card wasn't shown. Ivor Allchurch, a man with a very big reputation and a very big price tag, was seeing plenty of the ball, and it was my job to stop him. We were chatting away to each other, as was often the case, so I decided that the next time we came together it would be one that he wouldn't forget for a while. I can remember the incident quite clearly. Just as he took the ball under control, I was in to him, and he hit the floor with a terrible thud. The referee was on his whistle immediately, and I think he spoke to me for at least two minutes. It was such a bad tackle that even Billy Cush commented on it afterwards, when he said something like, 'Bloody hell Peter, has he been calling your mam or something.' It was a tough game, played by tough people, and Ivor was soon up and running around again, and we shook hands as if nothing had happened when we got to full time.

Also making his way in the team that season was a fantastic young player called Chris Crowe. He was a great inside right, a really creative user of the ball, and he had a wonderful first touch. I enjoyed playing with him immensely. Alan Shackleton used to take all of the praise for the goals that he scored, but much of the thanks for that had to go to Crowe. Jack Taylor eventually allowed him to leave the club in 1960, and that proved to be a real filip for Chris as his reputation grew overnight. He became a real favourite at Nottingham Forest and at Wolves, and he was rewarded with a full England cap in 1963.

Don't Shout at me Sergeant Major

I have already mentioned him briefly, but it's worth dwelling for a while on our team manager of four months, Bill Lambton. I believe that Bill had been a Sergeant Major in the Army and he introduced some crazy training methods almost from the moment he arrived. One morning we went over to Fullerton Park (now a car park) and we were confronted by a line of hurdles that he'd laid out before we got there. There were some grumbles as we waited to find out what he was up to, and the usual suspects took the opportunity to release some of the tension by winding up a few of the more fiery characters in the squad.

One of the most vocal of our group was a Scottish inside forward called George O'Brien. He had a knack of spotting who was the more likely to bite first, and then he would go for them until he got them to crack. One of his favourite targets was our small and stocky Irish international, Wilbur Cush. Wilbur, although not the biggest bloke you could ever hope to meet, was one of the best headers of the ball in the team, but that didn't stop his size from being the brunt of George's jokes. We all knew that Wilbur was due to be married, so George got himself alongside him as we went through the warm up, and asked him if it was going to be a top hat and tails affair. Wilbur took the bait and said yes, only for George to then ask him if he was having castors fitted to the tails to help him up the aisle on the big day. Poor old Wilbur was furious (he could be sensitive about his height if you caught him on the wrong day) but he couldn't do anything about it at the time. Lambton was marching around and barking his orders, and it was hard to keep the giggles down and pretend that we were taking things seriously with George clearly sensing that his wind up was doing the trick. By the time we were let loose on the hurdles Wilbur was at boiling point, so he got rid of his anger by crashing right through the middle of the lot of them. Needless to say that was the last time they were used as part of our training sessions – so well done Wilbur!

I think the powers that be at Elland Road quickly realised that things weren't working out with Bill Lambton, and he was asked to leave with no pomp or ceremony. He wasn't a bad man, and he could actually be quite a likeable character, but his methods were never going to work on professional footballers, so there were no real tears or feelings of regret when he moved on.

The first team trainer, Bob Roxburgh, stepped up to fill the void and, initially, that felt as bad for me as when Lambton was in charge. Bob had been my coach as a 15-year old, and he had scared the life out of me with his no-nonsense attitude. One of the things he used to make me do every morning, back when I was a kid, was go across the road and make sure that John Charles was out of bed. I always took a handful of pebbles with me, to throw up at his bedroom window but, for a spotty little youngster of that age, faced with a monster of an athlete like Charles, it was one hell of a nerve wracking experience. Once I'd finally raised him, and that could take anything up to half an hour, if not longer, he'd always greet me with a less than friendly 'GO AWAY' … or words to that effect. He did whatever he did to wake himself up, and by the time he got outside he was always extremely friendly and full of jokes, and it got to the point where I would actually look forward to carrying out my wake-up duties. To be fair to John, he seemed to remember me for my morning escapades, and years later he became one of my best friends.

I started to see more and more of Mary after our training sessions were over, which I was delighted about, so things were going really well for me in all areas of my life. It was around this time that I bought myself my first car. It was a black Morris Minor (registration number WTU 186 – how's that for a memory) and it used to have orange arms that appeared out of the side whenever you indicated to go left or right. How they survived without getting knocked off is anyone's guess, as they came out a fair old way once they were activated.

I took Mary to the cinema in it one night, parked the car on the car park, she put some of her stuff away in the glove compartment, and in we went to watch the film. When it was over we came out in to the cold night air and, ever the gentleman, I opened the door to let her in so that I could take her home. Whilst we were driving along she opened the drop down to retrieve her things and she became quite agitated. She said, 'Peter, that book I put in here has gone.' I asked her if she was joking, and she said no, so we both started to panic a bit. I had a quick look around, and it slowly started to dawn on me what had happened. I turned to her and said, 'Mary, you aren't going to believe this, but this isn't my car!' I'm sure you can imagine how shocked and terrified we were, so we drove back to the cinema and, fortunately, my own car was still sat there … exactly where we had left it by the way. I parked this other one up, and we quickly got in to mine and got out of there as fast as we could. My heart was racing at ten to the dozen, as I had visions of police cells and them looking at me as if I was some kind of idiot as they listened to what I'm sure they would have treated as a more than dubious story. That incident made us realise that the Morris Minor car keys were all the same, and that they would fit any car. We took a little bit more care about what we were doing with it from that moment on.

Room for a Big 'Un

One slight disappointment came along for me on a personal level during the late 1950's when my old room mate Dilwyn Jones got himself a transfer to Crewe Alexandra. We were close friends by then, and I knew that I was going to miss him, but the move was one that he needed to make if he was going to get first team football.

This sudden departure left an empty space in my room, and that was filled by a big Geordie lad called Jack Charlton. As we all know, Big Jack went on to great things for club and country but, when he first moved in with me, he was having rather a tough time of it. Most of the football he was playing was for the Reserves, because he was being kept out of the side by a steady performer called Jack Marsden. He probably still hadn't found his best position, and neither had the coaches, so his size meant that he would sometimes be played as a forward. He did it, but he wasn't comfortable with it, and the game would often pass him by as he tried to get more involved.

I wasn't really surprised by that because, and I think Jack would be the first to admit this himself, he didn't really seem to have his heart in it at that time. He could be very lazy if he didn't feel right, he was stubborn and, probably worst of all, he liked a pint or three.

His general routine for a Saturday night was to come in to the room after he'd had a few drinks, drag the gazunder out from under the bed (a pot that literally lived in the space between the bed and the floor), fill it, open the window and then empty it out on to the street. If that happened just the once, then we counted ourselves lucky. In those days we only had outside toilets, so there was absolutely no point in asking him to change his habits.

He also thought nothing of borrowing my clothes and, when I was away for whatever reason, it became a bit of a lottery as to what I would find when I got back. Another favourite of his was away games. Night porters at hotels back in those days would walk along the corridors and clean any shoes that were left outside a door. Big Jack used to take all of his and place whatever needed cleaning outside. As he always used to say, 'They aren't going to get done otherwise man, Peter!'

One trick that he used to get away with more times than I care to remember was with his cigarettes. He would make sure that he had two packets with him, at all times. One would be nearly full, and the other would have just one left in it. If anyone asked him for a cigarette, he would pull out the packet that had just one in it and say, 'Oh, sorry mate, that's all I've got left.' Usually, because he was so likeable, they would then offer him one of theirs, and he had the cheek to accept it. John Charles watched this and, I have to say, learned from it as instead of challenging Jack about it, he actually started doing it for himself.

A very poignant moment I remember with him was one day in 1958, when we came back in from an afternoon training session. We were laughing and joking as usual, but that changed quickly when news came through of the Munich air crash. Jack was not what you would call an emotional person, but he looked ashen when the implications of the news started to sink in. All I could do was wish him luck as he threw a suitcase together, and I am unsure to this day as to whether he drove to Manchester or up to Newcastle to be with his mother, Cissie. We were all thankful to hear that his brother Bobby was one of the survivors, but that did little to dampen the loss that was felt as the names of those who had died were released. One of my good friends from my days in the army was one of those, and it really did put things in perspective. We called him 'Snake Hips Eddie Colman,' and he was our camp rat catcher, and a very good one at that. He was wonderful company on any long journey, in particular when we travelled together from Leeds to Manchester on our way home, so it hurt to find out that he was gone.

The turning point not only for Jack, but for the whole club, was the appointment of Don Revie as manager, and I'll talk more about the circumstances behind that appointment in a moment. Along with his coaches Les Cocker and Syd Owen, he brought in a whole new and different way of doing things. Jack, like many of the other players, responded to it and we suddenly started to see the best of them. It's probably also worth mentioning that he'd just met his future wife, Pat, around this time and she also went a long way towards calming him down and pointing him in the right direction.

My own relationship with Mary was a really close one by now, and I decided that I wanted nothing other than for us to be man and wife. We got married at St Wilfred's Church in Farnley on June 20th 1959, and I thought that it was a marvellous occasion. Dilwyn came back over to be my best man, and I can honestly say that it was one of the proudest days of my life. I felt like the cat who had got the cream as I walked down the aisle with Mary on my arm, and it was good to see so many of our friends and relations also having a good time.

Back on the pitch we were starting to get a strong squad together, and it was getting harder to enjoy any kind of run in the first team. We were attracting people like Colin Grainger, a left winger from Sunderland who went on to score twice on his England debut at Wembley, and players of that stature were almost an automatic first choice on the team sheet.

As a slight aside, Colin was an excellent singer, and he actually sang in front of a packed crowd at the London Palladium. There was one unbelievable night when I found out that he was appearing at a club in Manchester, so I purchased a ticket for ten bob (equivalent of 50p in today's money) and settled down to watch him in action. Also on the bill that evening was a group of four boys from Liverpool, called the Beatles, who were causing a bit of a stir in music circles, and I have to say that they were fantastic to listen to live. Two weeks after I'd seen them they went to number one in the pop charts, so it's good to think that I was there just as it was all taking off for them.

Jack's the Lad

Bob Roxburgh wasn't in the hot seat for long at all because, and yet again, the club were looking for more than they felt they would get with him at the helm, and they appointed Jack Taylor to replace him for the start of the 1959/60 season. He was a very quiet and considered man – possibly too quiet, if we're being honest – but he definitely had an eye for a good player. Norman Hunter may be one who would disagree with that assessment though, as he never got on with Jack, and it's probably fair to say that Norman may have had to leave Elland Road had Mr Taylor kept hold of his job. Yet again Leeds fans can thank their lucky stars that things turned out as they did, or they would never have had the pleasure of watching Norman when he was at his best.

We had a South African winger called Gerald Francis with us who, like me, had been on the fringes of the first team for a couple of seasons. He was a quiet lad, and I liked him a lot because of the way that he used to just keep his head down and work. Albert Johanesson is often wrongly credited with being the first black player ever to turn out for Leeds, but it was definitely Gerry. He was a thrilling player to watch, and he scored some spectacular goals, but the lack of consistency in team selection affected him quite badly under Jack Taylor, and he was never really given the chance to shine that season. I always felt that was a shame, as he had plenty to offer, as he showed the following year when Taylor finally started to pick him more regularly.

One of the best signings that Jack ever made was a young man called Don Revie, who came in from Sunderland at a cost of £12,000. He was a lovely footballer, a good passer of the ball and a great communicator out on the pitch, and he was a pleasure to know and to play beside.

A game that stands out for me that we played in together, now that I come to think about it, was a meeting with FA Cup finalists Nottingham Forest not long after Don had taken over as our captain. I don't mind saying that we ran the show between us, and Don created two of Alan Shackleton's goals, with me making another one for him, as he grabbed a hat-trick in a comfortable 3-0 away win.

Another of Taylor's signings was John McCole, a very athletic Scottish centre forward. He was one of those rarities in the game in that he was almost guaranteed to get you 20 goals a season, and he could strike the ball cleanly with either foot. He had the nickname of 'Four Goal McCole' and I don't recall that he ever achieved that feat with Leeds, so I can only think that he did it at Bradford City, which is where Jack Taylor found him.

Despite this seemingly never-ending procession of good players, we struggled terribly and we slipped towards what became an almost inevitable relegation. We won just seven games after Christmas, and Jack never really had the personality or the charisma to lift the dressing room. I can look back now and see, in my mind's eye, the quality of the players that we had in and around the first team and there is just no way that we should have found ourselves in that position. We could score goals, we had some very solid midfielders and we had a great team spirit, but we just couldn't halt the run of bad results, no matter what we did. It goes without saying that we were all gutted at how things turned out, but it was more a feeling of frustration that engulfed us than anything else. Like I say, we shouldn't have been down there in the first place.

Make Way for the Don

Life in Division 2 was a very rude awakening for us, and it turned out to be anything but the romp back towards the promotion and wild celebrations that some of those behind the scenes at the club, and certainly the fans, expected. We were in amongst some very big name clubs, and others who had been established at that level and amongst that very different style of football for years, and the competition was fierce. Derby County, Ipswich Town and Liverpool were all there in the mix, and they were as desperate for promotion in to the top flight as anyone. We really struggled to impose ourselves if truth be known, and it was rarely that we managed to string a succession of victories together.

As an example of how tough things were on the football side of life, even a player like Don Revie only managed something like 15 appearances, as Jack Taylor tinkered and fiddled with his team selection in an attempt to find the winning combination.

Our real problem was the fact that we couldn't stop leaking silly goals, so it didn't really matter that we were able to score them ourselves. As the season went on, and as we floated around the lower mid-table positions, rumours began to grow that the board were unhappy, and the players began to openly talk about Jack's future in the dressing room.

I was sat in the communal bath with Don Revie at Elland Road one day along with another good friend of ours called Jimmy Ashall, following one of our longer training sessions, and Don took me by surprise when he asked me, out of the blue, whether I fancied moving to Bournemouth with him. I don't think I said too much, because I was trying to work out what he meant, so he went on to explain that they had been in touch to offer him the player-manager post. He made it clear that he wanted me to go with him, if he took the job, and that I would also get first team football from the moment I signed the contract.

Initially I thought that it might be part of a wind up, but he soon convinced me that he was being serious and that he was tempted to agree to the terms that were on offer. I did all that I could do when faced with a question like that, and I told him that I'd think about it.

For me, I have to say that I found it to be an interesting proposition. I could see all of the plus points, with the main one being that I was going to be playing football every week. However, I also had Mary to consider, and I knew that she was very close to her mother, and that she would find it very difficult to move such a long way away. I have no doubt that she would have followed me if I'd decided that it was what I wanted, but I'm not sure that I could have done that to her unless it was absolutely necessary. As far as I was concerned, we were a team, and there was no way that I wanted to do anything without considering all of the implications, and without hearing what she had to say. As it was, she went very quiet when I told her about it, and I think I knew then that she was worried about the distance involved, and what that would mean.

I went in to training the next morning with very mixed feelings. I think I had already decided to say no, but I knew that Don would have plenty to say to me, and that he would try to persuade me to go with him, and I wasn't sure how I was going to react to that at all. There was no sign of Don when I got to the changing rooms, but nobody had really noticed that and the banter carried on as usual as we went about the business of getting ourselves ready. Just as we were finishing off we were told to sit down and wait, because the club chairman wanted to speak to us. We all knew what that meant, because we had been struggling under Jack Taylor and, as I say, we had been wondering out loud as to how long it was going to be allowed to continue.

When what happened next happened, you could have knocked me down with a feather. Mr Reynolds the chairman walked in and solemnly announced that Jack had indeed been relieved of his position. He then went on to say that the club had already found his successor, and that it was a man that he was certain we would all find to be a popular replacement. He then pointed at Don and said, 'Gentleman, Don Revie is your new manager.' I was both stunned and delighted. Going from talking to him in the communal bath to calling him Boss took a bit of getting used to, but he had that air about him that left no doubt who was in charge, and we all fell quickly in to place. Obviously Mary was over the moon when I told her later that day, because it meant that we no longer had to make the Bournemouth decision, and I was pleased on a personal level because Don was an excellent coach. He had been fantastic with me, helping me to develop all manner of things within all areas of my game, and I could see only good times ahead with him in charge.

As I mentioned earlier, he had beside him two fantastic coaches in Syd Owen and Les Cocker. They were chalk and cheese, but together they covered just about everything. Of the pair, Syd was the disciplinarian. He didn't care who you were, if he felt that you weren't pulling your weight, or that you were messing around too much, then he would tell you, and you'd know that you'd just been told off as well! Les was the one that you could talk to, if you needed to, but, having said that, he was still a man who could turn the screw if and when he needed to.

There was a good feeling about the place with the three of them in charge, but we were still really worried that the appointment of Revie might just have come a few weeks too late, as we still weren't clear of relegation. As it was we had enough of a cushion to see ourselves through, and the final league table made it look much more comfortable than it actually was.

I finally got myself a goal for the club towards the end of that season, and not long after Don had taken over. The fans must have been at the end of their tether because, with just three games left to play, we finally showed them what we could do. Admittedly our opponents Lincoln were in dire straits at the foot of the table but it was men against boys as McCole and Bremner ran the show. I pitched in with the seventh goal in a 7-0 home win, and it was a wonderful moment for me, even though it had felt like a very long time in coming.

13

New Faces Arrive

We went in to the 1961/62 season with very high hopes, and it looked encouraging as we won our first two games comfortably. The optimism was short-lived, however, as the old defensive frailties returned to haunt us.

Don, in a similar way to Jack Taylor before him, found that it was difficult to find his best starting eleven, and he began to look around in the transfer market. Whilst that was ongoing, he gave me a start against Huddersfield Town in a League Cup game, and it was probably one of my best performances in a Leeds shirt. Most of the good stuff that we played came through me, and I got myself another goal for my tally as we huffed and puffed our way to a 3-2 victory. Even after performances like that Don would still remain tight-lipped, never indicating either one way or the other as to how he felt that you had played. I have to be honest and say that I missed enough chances to have won the game ten times over, but I kept going and I got my reward when I grabbed the winner with a 25-yard shot that had Billy Bremner jumping around with excitement.

That was another of those games, by the way, where we all found ourselves out on the pitch before kick off, with shovels and brushes, when the heavens opened and about three feet of snow dumped itself onto Elland Road. It was no easy task to get rid of it, but everyone mucked in and the game went ahead, as scheduled.

I was picked to play the following week, against Plymouth, and off I went on a run of three goals in four games as I set out to make myself an automatic choice every week. It was actually Don who set up one of my favourite Leeds goals when we travelled to play Swansea at Vetch Field, late in October. The Swans had a couple of ex-Manchester United players in their ranks, and it was a game that was never going to be an easy ride for us. They were pressing forward during the first half hour, and I had taken a kick on the shin from their outside left, a lad called Morgan, so I was still quite high up the pitch when Revie intercepted a pass and looked up to see what his options were. I waved for it, and he put it in just the right place so that I was able to run on and slot it underneath their keeper, to give us the lead. They kicked us all over the pitch after that, but we gave as good as we got, and we held on to take the points and a very well earned victory.

There was a particularly nice moment after I scored the goal that earned us a point against Southampton at Elland Road. At the end of the game I had arranged to meet Billy Bremner in the car park, and whilst I was waiting for him a group of fans came across to shake my hand and thank me for what I had done. That was good, because we were going through some tough times, and it could often feel that the whole world was against you.

Don was soon given permission to take a dip in to the transfer fund in a bid to turn things round for us. He wanted to bring more steel in to the team, so one of his first signings was a terrier from Celtic called Eric Smith. Eric trained in exactly the same way that he played, and he was responsible for us taking the decision to wear shin pads during our 5-a-side sessions, something that we had never done before. An added bonus with Eric was that he bought and sold cars during his spare time, so he was never short of a good deal on the latest model.

Freddie Goodwin was next to arrive, from Manchester United, and he was a player that I had admired for a while, but I always felt that I was better and had more to offer than he did. Unfortunately for me both Eric and Freddie were wing halves, and they were players that Don had paid money for, so I really started to fear for my future.

Revie also secured the signing of Scottish international keeper Tommy Younger. Tommy was another real character to have around, and he became noted for his preference for King Edward cigars. We always wondered how he could afford them, because they weren't cheap even in those days, until one day we rumbled him. He seemed to receive packages regularly, and he would never let on as to what they were, but one of the lads spotted that the post mark was from America. It turned out that he was importing his cigars in bulk, and on the cheap, from across the Atlantic. His cigar smoking lost some of its mystery from that day forth.

Of all of the signings that Don made I would say that the biggest and best was wee Bobby Collins. There is no doubt in my mind at all that he made a significant impact and that he had a massive influence on the success that Revie was subsequently allowed to go on and enjoy. We were looking odds on for relegation before Collins came in, but he provided the spark that was needed and the results began to improve.

Don had his own quirks, as does everybody, and he could be very, very superstitious, particularly if the team had just won, and I remember that he once told me off because I had put my boots on the treatment table in the middle of the dressing room. I received a lengthy lecture on how much bad luck it could bring to do that, and all the while all I wanted to do was get hold of the boots and put them on the floor, just to shut him up.

Also, if we did win a game, he would put the suit that he had been wearing to one side, and he would wear it for the next match as well. Obviously, when I was at the club, that meant that he was at the tailor for a new one every week, but that soon changed once the likes of Bremner and Hunter came to the fore. He must have had the same one on for about four months when his team started to weave its magic, because they used to go on some fantastic unbeaten runs.

Back to our own battle against the drop, and we were due to play Bury towards the end of the season, where Bob Stokoe was their no-nonsense player-manager at centre half. It turned out that Don knew him to speak to quite well, and Bury were safe at the time, so Don took it upon himself to go in and say hello to Bob when we got to the ground. I have no idea what happened between the pair, but there were some really harsh words exchanged and they never spoke to each other again afterwards. They didn't even look at each other or shake hands when the final whistle went so whatever it was that had caused the rift, it must have been serious. As it was Big Jack earned us a point in the game, and we ended the campaign with a nine match unbeaten run that just about kept our heads above water.

14

One of a Kind

Don Revie is one of those men that I could talk about for hours. He was one of a kind, and some of the things he introduced were way ahead of his time. For example, he was a wonderful golfer, with a single figure handicap, and he always used golf as his treat to the squad if we had a good result at the weekend. He'd arrange for everyone to go for a round at Moortown Golf Club, where he was a member, and that used to go down extremely well, because there were some very good golfers in the dressing room at that time.

However, even though I love the game now, I couldn't get away with it at all during my younger days. To me it was a waste of a good walk. I'm pleased to say that Billy Bremner felt exactly the same way about it, so we used to make sure that we were paired together for one of the final tee-off times whenever the team was booked to play. We'd set ourselves up, go through the motions, and as soon as the group in front disappeared out of sight we would run back to the club house, put our clubs away and play snooker all day. Don never found out, and neither did any of the other lads, as we used to make up stories about amazing shots and hole-in-one near misses so that we didn't stand out.

If he felt that we needed a break or a change of scenery he would arrange a trip across to Blackpool, and we would play on the Championship course out at Lytham. That was a very high standard of golf course, and the rest of the lads used to get excited about it, but Billy and I used to just look at each other and raise our eyebrows in disgust. What I will say, though, is that everything was laid on when we had trips like that. Food, golf, drinks, and accommodation – everything was paid for by Leeds United. I do feel guilty for not appreciating that more than I did because, as I say, the first thing that Billy and I did was look for a way out of it so that we could crack on and do our own thing.

With all of the new signings that he'd made I found that I was scrapping for a starting place, but I was still getting the odd run out, and I felt that I was performing quite well. I remember playing in a 1-0 victory over Southampton and supplying a ball in to the box from which my best pal Billy Bremner scored the winner. Thinking about it now, it probably looked like a superb piece of football, and the newspaper reports afterwards described it as a 'slide rule pass from McConnell.' What they didn't realise is that it was actually a shot, but I'd got it completely and woefully wrong, to say the least. Billy knew, of course, but he kept his mouth shut and let me take the praise. Don, on the other hand, simply gave me a wink, and I was never certain if that was to tell me well done, or because he had also sussed the truth behind my wonderful, defence splitting moment of inspiration.

He was also the only manager that I have ever played under who would tell you that you hadn't been selected to play before the team sheet went up. That was a measure of the kind of person that he was, in all honesty. Unless you were one of the team superstars, you could never really second guess what he was thinking about team selection, so him taking the time do that was appreciated by everybody. It wasn't all good, though, because we soon became aware of the procedure. If you weren't in his team for that week, he would send for you, so we used to dread getting that call. I was always very impressed with the way that he handled those situations though. He would never give you an excuse, it was always a reason why, so you left his office knowing what his thoughts were and why he'd gone with the selection that he'd made. I'm not saying that we agreed with him every time, but at least he made sure that there was no doubt and no tittle-tattle. Under every other manager, we used to have to wait until Friday morning when the team sheet would go up on the notice board in the player's corridor. It was only then that you found out whether you were playing or not and there was rarely an explanation offered.

I still regard him as the best of the managers that I worked under, and I had the honour of working with some good ones, so it was a shame that things didn't really go for him when he got the England position. He eventually took the job over in the Emirates, and I think the only reason that he accepted that was because he felt that he was going to be asked to leave by the FA anyway.

As a club manager, he was brilliant. He was almost like a father to everybody, and he liked to make sure that his players were informed about his decisions, and the reasons he did things, as much as he possibly could.

He introduced things like games of bingo and carpet bowls before a game, to try to foster the team spirit and camaraderie, and these may have been little things but it was a whole new way of thinking that, as I said earlier, just hadn't been seen before. He also had a new gadget fitted in the dressing room that gave the players what was called an aqua-massage after every game, and that proved to be quite popular … after a while. Basically a Jacuzzi, it would whip the bath water up in to a frenzy, sending bubbles everywhere, but it was extremely relaxing after 90 minutes of hard, competitive football.

To show the way he used to think, there was one occasion, when we played Portsmouth away, that I got myself injured and I had to be carried off the field for treatment. I had clashed heads with their inside forward, and there was blood pouring out of a very deep wound. Revie had just changed us to the Real Madrid strip, so we were wearing all-white, and mine turned red within a matter of seconds. I wasn't knocked unconscious, or anything like that, but I was stunned and extremely dizzy for a few moments. Les Cocker was busy with his sponge when little Billy ran over, had a good look at it and then said, 'Bloody hell Les that's one of the worst I've ever seen.' He gave me a wink and ran away, and I fell back down again feeling really sorry for myself. There were no subs back then, so Don shoved me out on to the right wing for the second half and I had nine stitches, a plaster over my eye and a sponge so that I could keep wiping the blood away. By the time I got home I looked like Henry Cooper, because my eye had swollen shut and there was a lovely big bruise all down one side of my face.

Now, there used to be a sports paper published in Leeds within moments of the full time whistle going, and that would usually have the full match details in it. For some reason, the report on our game stopped at half time in this particular issue. All that Mary and my mum had seen back home in Leeds was that I had been stretchered off. There was no explanation as to why I'd been injured, no follow up on whether I had come back on or not, absolutely nothing. Don found out that this had happened when we got back to Elland Road and he knew that they would have been worried about me so, the next morning, he was on our doorstep with a box of chocolates and a bunch of flowers for the wife. She thought that was fantastic, and that's exactly why he used to do things like that, so that the wives and families would know that the club valued them for the sacrifices that they had to make.

On the subject of injuries, I learned a real lesson when we played Leicester City on a Tuesday night, when I was still just 21 years old. During the game I was chasing after the ball and I felt a little twinge in the back of my leg. I didn't think much of it, but I mentioned it to one of the coaches after the game, because it started to tighten up a bit. They took me in to the treatment room the next morning and confirmed that I'd pulled my hamstring. They gave me a few exercises to do and then told me to be ready for a fitness test on the Friday morning, because we were due to travel down to play West Ham on the Saturday. I was worried, because I'd just got in to the team and it was the first time that I'd been able to enjoy a decent run of games.

When the Friday came I went down to the training ground for my test, did a few exercises and some sprints, and I declared myself fit. Ten minutes in to the game the next day, it might even have been less than that, I felt an almighty tug and a sudden burst of pain behind my knee. My hamstring had gone, and I ended up sitting on the sidelines for six weeks. I rushed myself back, to take part in a Reserve game, and the same thing happened to me again. I missed twelve weeks in total, and that was all through me being young, headstrong and plain daft.

By now Debra Mary, our first daughter, had been born. Mary and I had moved to Waincliffe Drive in Leeds, and I think we were both ready for a baby and, indeed, we'd actually hinted about trying a number of times. Revie was one of the first to send us congratulations, but he was trumped on this occasion by Billy Bremner. He was there to visit us the moment we got home from hospital and he held in his hands possibly the biggest teddy bear I had ever seen (bigger than him, in fact), and his face sported a smile to match it. It actually meant a lot to us that he had taken the time to come over and make sure that we were all alright, so the least I could do was assist him in wetting the babies head!

Billy and I had become close friends from the first day that he had arrived from Stirling. We used to play snooker and table tennis together all the time, and I was there with him when he bought his first car, a really flashy Vauxhall Victor that was one of THE cars to have back in those days.

I used to tease Billy constantly after I moved to Carlisle, because he was switched to play in my position shortly after I left the club. Whenever I saw him I said something along the lines of, 'Billy, no one would ever have heard of you if I had stayed here at Elland Road. You'd never have got my shirt.' It always brought a smile to his face and, funnily enough, he never really argued against it either!

15

Another Decision to Make

Back to Don Revie, and most of my time football wise under him was
spent on the sidelines or in the Reserves, and I found that to be agony.
I started to wonder if I would ever get a regular place again when I got
a message telling me that I had to pop along to the manager's office.
When I got there he told me that Ivor Powell had been in touch and
that he had expressed an interest in taking me over to Carlisle. Don
asked me what I thought about it, then immediately told me that he
was reluctant to let me go anyway, at least until that weeks Reserve
game had been played.

Anyway, as it happens, that interest appeared to die for a short while
and I found myself back in the first team for the trip across to
Deepdale to play Preston. They had a player called Peter Thompson
out on the left (Thompson later went on to be a big success at Anfield),
and Revie gave me the job of stopping him from playing. He used to
like to drop his shoulder and come inside on his right foot, and I was
given specific instructions to make sure that I didn't allow that to
happen. The game couldn't have gone any better for me, with
Thompson getting little opportunity to shine, and all of my team mates
congratulated me at the end. As we got to the tunnel Bobby Collins put
his arm round me and said, 'Nice one Peter, there's no way he can
drop you after that.'

Don didn't really say much to me after the game, so I left it at that and
hoped that I'd done enough to give him something to think about. I got
myself changed, threw my kit together and then made my way out of
the building, towards the bus, so I could get settled in for the journey
back to Leeds. As I closed the outside door I heard a voice behind me
whisper, 'Peter, Peter, come over here.' At first I thought it was someone
after an autograph or a chat about the game, but as I got closer I

realised that it was Ivor Powell. He'd dressed himself up in a flat cap, which he'd pulled down over his brow, and a big trench coat that had the collar up to hide his face. He looked exactly like Inspector Clouseau.

So, in the middle of the coach park at Preston he proceeded to tell me what was on offer at Carlisle. He told me that he would give me a club house, rent free, a pay rise and, most significantly, that he wanted to make me his team captain straight away. I played it cool, told him that I'd think about it, and I made my way on to the bus with a little more to think about than I'd had when I'd climbed out of the bath half an hour earlier.

Later that week Don called me down to his office again and he told me that Carlisle United had made a formal offer, and that Leeds were willing to accept it if I decided that I wanted to move. I agreed to go and talk to Ivor but, having already had the terms of the deal given to me at Preston, it made the whole thing a bit of a formality.

The rest, as they say, is history … and it really is history because Leeds went from strength to strength almost from the moment I left. Was that coincidence or was it all down to my departure – I suppose we'll never really know for sure! Seriously though, the move turned out to be the best thing that could have happened for me as I went on to enjoy some wonderful years with Carlisle, and I was also able to sit back and watch the success that my good friends over at Elland Road were beginning to enjoy.

Just before I moved away from Leeds my younger brother, Barry, came across to stay with us. He was a superb footballer in his own right and I know that he could have gone on to make it in the game if things had turned out differently. Only he will be able to explain fully what happened, but I think he missed home and his girlfriend, and he decided that it wasn't for him. He later played for Buxton in the Cheshire League, and was very successful for them, as well as doing a full time job as a printer for the Daily Express. Come to think of it, he was probably earning more than me at the time.

There were times, just before I made the move to Cumbria, for example, when I did wonder whether it would be a better decision for me to remain at Elland Road and fight for my place. As bad luck would have it, about three weeks after I left Freddie Goodwin broke his leg and was ruled out long term and then, amazingly, Eric Smith suffered the same injury within the space of a fortnight. That meant that there were two half back positions vacant, and I know for a fact that, had I still been there, I'd have stepped up to fill one of them. It was at that point that Don Revie was forced in to making Billy Bremner's move from number 7 to number 4 a permanent one. As we all know, Billy took to it like a duck to water, and his legend was born.

When I moved back to Leeds, after I had retired from the game, I used to do the commentary for the games with Barney Colehan and a local car trader called Tommy Kneeshaw. Billy Bremner was manager at the time, and I would make my way down to his office at full time to say hello and to talk about old times. I was always made to feel very welcome by the club, and that is something that I will always appreciate.

16

A Last Word About Billy

One of my favourite Billy Bremner stories comes from when we invited him to speak at a dinner event at my dad's Working Men's Club in Manchester, along with a boxer called John H Stracey. The rivalry between the two cities, and particularly the Manchester United and Leeds United football clubs, was as intense then as it's ever been, so most of the audience started waving their red serviettes at him as soon as he stood up to do his bit. He quickly won them over when he told them a story about a game that he had been involved in at Old Trafford. Nobby Stiles had gone in for a challenge with Big Jack just before half time, and he'd sent the big man flying with the force of the tackle. Jack had stood up, strode after him and had literally grabbed him by the scruff of the neck. Just as he had started launching in to a tirade Nobby had put his hands out, as if he was blind, and had said, 'Oh, is that you Jack, I'd wondered what it was that I'd banged in to. Can you give me a hand a moment, I seem to have lost my contact lenses.' The way Billy told that story brought the house down, and they soon forgot their rivalries.

It was a really good night all round, and Billy's turn at speaking was followed by Stracey. One of his stories was about when he was fighting for the welterweight title over in America against Carlos Palomino. He'd been knocked all over the ring for five rounds, been given a real pounding, and he had suffered a broken nose and all kinds of damage to his body. He went back to his corner at the end of the fifth round and his trainer had said to him, 'You're doing a great job here John, he's hardly laid a glove on you.' John had spat the blood out of his mouth and said, 'Well keep an eye on that ****** referee then will you, because somebody is giving me a right good kicking here!'

I found out about Billy's death when I came back from a family holiday. We were busy unpacking so I had turned the TV on in the background, to catch up with the news. There at the bottom of the screen was a scrolling news flash saying that Billy had died. It took a while for it to sink in, because he was such a bubbly young man, and I had to sit down as the enormity of the whole thing hit me squarely between the eyes.

I can remember some of the battles he had out on the pitch, because he could be a hard little man when he had to be. Dave Mackay of Tottenham was exchanging blows with him in one game, and I think they still play video footage to this day of the fight that he had with Kevin Keegan at Wembley.

It's no wonder that his statue is outside the ground, because he really was one of the all-time greats. The spirit that he brought to that Leeds team was immeasurable.

Billy was a very sad loss, because I had been through so much with him, but I was impressed when Sir Alex Ferguson turned up at his funeral in Doncaster, to pay his respects. Sir Alex had been in Italy the night before to watch his own side play Juventus, but he had cut in to his itinerary to fly back to Manchester and then drive across the country to make sure he could be there. It was an extremely emotional occasion, and I think we were all in tears when Billy's close friend Alan Clarke struggled to get his words out when he went up to the pulpit. The turn out of former players on the day was testament to his character, and his poor wife Vicky was naturally grief stricken. Every time I pass his statue at Elland Road I feel choked, but I also remember the good times and the mischief that he used to get up to, and I am honoured to have known him and to have been close to him.

I was talking to Eddie Gray at my local golf course recently, and he stunned me when he mentioned that it is now ten years since Billy passed away. He was 54 when he died, and we both agreed that it was a real shame that we had lost him at such a young age. We soon got to talking about some of the stuff that Billy used to get up to, and it reminded us just how much of a character he was. He had a real guardian angel in Don Revie because I think the manager helped him out of some tricky situations on a number of occasions. Don absolutely adored him, and he made sure that he was very well looked after.

Billy liked a cigarette and he liked a drink, but not necessarily in that order, and there was one occasion when he and Eddie had travelled up to Scotland for an international game against Holland. They'd gone in Billy's new car, a brand new bright orange sports car type thing that was typical of the kind of man that he was. The Dutch were one of the best sides in the world at the time, but the Scottish lads had played out of their skins and had beaten them, so they decided that they'd celebrate afterwards. Eddie stayed on the soft drinks, always wary of what Billy might do, and it turned out to be a good decision because he was the one who had to drive back down to Leeds, with Billy fast asleep from the moment he sat in the passenger seat! Eddie had taken Billy back to his own house in Wetherby, knowing full well that Billy's wife would have gone mad if he'd returned home in that state. Mind you, he was bright as a button for training the next day, because he was one of those lads who could have a heavy night and still turn it on once there was work to be done, so he got away with it in the end.

It was Bremner who saddled me with the nickname of Columbo for a while, and all because I'd bought myself what I considered to be a very nice new raincoat. The first time he saw it he grabbed the rest of the lads and said, 'Hey, has there been a murder around here somewhere or something, they've sent that American detective fella to sort us out.'

Can you imagine a Leeds United team without Billy and Bobby Collins driving them on? What a pair, and what a joy for the fans to watch. Other supporters, along with some sections of the media, gave them the name of 'Dirty Leeds' but that has never really rung true with me at all. They were a formidable side and they had everything in their locker. They wanted to play football, but if they had to battle, then battle they would. I can still remember the 5-0 home win over Southampton when cries of 'Ole' accompanied a string of 35 consecutive passes, and you have to admire the fact that most of Don Revie's team in that game had come from players who had made their way through the Youth system.

Whatever it was that gave Don the ability to spot a player who would make things happen, it was uncanny. I could sit here and list them all day – Sprake, Reaney, Cooper, Charlton, Bremner, Hunter, Gray, Lorimer, Yorath, Bates – some of these guys were second to none. As time went on they brought in Johnny Giles, a football artist if ever there was one; Mick Jones, a very under rated centre forward and a work horse who did a lot of the hard stuff for Alan Clarke. For Leeds fans these were great years, and they were able to enjoy a dominant period thanks to wonderful players who played for each other and who brought pride and success to a club that had been on the brink of something big for decades.

A Real Gentleman

As I say, the move across to Cumbria was all thanks to the Carlisle manager at the time, Ivor Powell. It took a little bit of adjusting to because it was a smaller ground, a smaller kitty and the facilities were often whatever we ourselves could scratch together, but I quickly learned that they were some of the most loyal supporters in the country.

As for Ivor, he had been one of my coaches in my younger days and he had made me captain of the Youth and second teams during his time at Leeds. He was fanatical about football and one of the most enthusiastic men I have ever come across. Everything with him was to be done well, done now, and done better next time, and I can honestly say that he gave me an excellent grounding in the game. He was also incredibly experienced, having played for and captained Wales and, as young lads, we would never tire of listening to what he had to say.

I had and still do have a huge amount of respect for him, and I was delighted for him when he was chosen to receive an MBE for his services to football. I just hope he didn't have to speak to the Queen when he went to meet her, because he had a terrible habit of making statements that were never quite right, even though you always knew what he was getting at.

For example, we were losing 2-0 to Barnsley once and he told us at half time, 'Why don't you lot take a leaf out of their book, every Tom, Dick and Angle is having a shot, and they're in front because of it.' On one of our away trips he had booked us in to see the latest blockbuster at the cinema, so he said, 'Hurry up and finish your tea lads, we're off to see a hysterical film called Ben Hur.' Probably the funniest, from what was a really sad situation, was when he walked in to the dressing room and we could tell that he wasn't his usual self. Someone asked him if he was alright and he replied, 'No, it's horrible, the wife's mother has just died and she is laid at home prostitute with grief.' It was all we could do not to laugh out loud at him, because he never had any idea that he was making these mistakes and, of course, that just made the whole thing even funnier for us. That was all just a part of who he was, though, and it made him even more likeable as a person.

I understand that he is still coaching down in Bath, and I know that they will love him down there. He is as honest as the day is long, and he is the kind of person who would never ask anyone to do anything that he couldn't do, or hadn't already done, himself.

There was one day, when we were in the gym, that he took it upon himself to coach Joe Livingstone on how to generate more power with his neck muscles when heading a ball. As I've already said elsewhere, the balls were heavy leather objects back then, with thick laces down one side, so it was no mean feat to get the thing to zip through the air, especially from a standing jump. Joe and Ivor went at their practice for a good twenty minutes until they finally decided that they'd had enough. When I spotted that they were walking off I shouted at Ivor and asked him for one more demonstration. He looked at my hands, noticed that I'd picked up a medicine ball (they weighed about 7lbs) instead of a football and he must have decided that it was some kind of challenge. Without batting an eyelid he said, 'Come on then,' and he headed the damn thing back towards me when I threw it. Anyone else would have been knocked backwards, but not our Ivor!

Making a Mark

Although the gates were only averaging around the 5000 mark when I arrived in 1962, there was still plenty of passion and noise from the terraces. The standing areas for the fans were made up of old railway sleepers and cinders, and there was a flimsy wooden fence, for want of a better way of describing it, that went round the perimeter of the pitch.

The playing surface itself was surprisingly good, meaning that we could play our passing game and keep the ball on the floor. That was important to Ivor because he liked his teams to do things the right way, and that was something that all of his players appreciated.

My debut for United was a home game against Queens Park Rangers and Ivor gave me the number 6 shirt. I can't say that I was overly happy about that, but I had my work cut out if I wanted to displace a real Carlisle hero called Ginger Thompson, who played in my favoured position. In a sport full of strong, athletic people, Ron was up there with the strongest of them. He was a part time player for us, and he filled up the rest of his week as a builder around the City. He used to terrorise David Oliphant on the team bus, if he was in a playful mood, because Ollie was fairly small in stature and would generally react if there was a wind up on the go. Ginger would pin him down, and do allsorts to him, but Ollie would never let up, giving as good as he got, and we would be in stitches as the pair of them battled away on the back seats.

Up front we had a local plumber called George Walker, so if there was ever any trouble around the house we were pretty much sorted with the pair of them. We only ever saw them on match days and for the Tuesday and Thursday evening training sessions, but they were never found wanting and were amongst the fittest members of the squad.

The fact that Ginger was wearing the shirt that I wanted to wear meant that I settled much slower than I would otherwise have wanted to. Some sections of the supporters were openly questioning me as a signing in those early weeks, and it was not the smooth transition that I had anticipated when I first agreed to come to the club. The problem I was having was that, being naturally right footed, I was obviously much more comfortable when playing on the right. I also liked to get forward and support the strikers as much as I could but, with the players that we had there at the time, I was being asked to play a much more defensive role over in the left half position. At times it felt really uncomfortable, and the crowd quickly picked up on that.

As a team, we weren't quite there, and we suffered some ridiculous results. We lost 5-2 at home to Bristol City, mostly because of a dire second half where we couldn't seem to keep the ball, and our supporters were none too pleased about that. There were some very cutting comments made as we left the pitch and walked towards the tunnel at full time and, I have to say, I think I agreed with just about everything that was said.

As with any player who goes through those periods, all you can do is knuckle down and keep working hard, and make sure that the belief in your own ability is always there. You do hear the comments from the crowd, because some of them can be quite vocal, but it's important not to let that affect you too much. I'm pleased to say that once I moved across to my rightful place in the half back line I never really looked back, and I think the fans were then able to see what it was I could do.

I was in Leeds before my first away match with the club, at Peterborough, to sort a few things out, so I arranged to be picked up by the team coach in Wetherby, at the King George Hotel car park. As far as hotels go, it was extremely impressive, and it was the kind of venue that Leeds would have used for their pre-match meals. I should really have taken a hint with what happened next because, when the bus pulled in, they took one look at the place and then headed across the road to a transport café for pie and peas. Anyway, I didn't really take that on board so, on the way home, I was slightly more impressed when we pulled in to a swanky hotel for something to eat. Our trainer, and a real character, was a man called Dick Young, and he just didn't suffer fools at all. He was one of the old fashioned style of coaches who had strict principles and methods, and I didn't really know what to make of him during my first few weeks at the club. It was only when I got to know him better, and as a person, that I realised just how much of a gem Carlisle United had found for themselves.

He brought me down to earth quickly on this occasion though when we all sat round the table for our meal. I was about two places down from Dick when the waiter came to take our orders. I looked at the menu and, with everyone sitting there quietly, I asked for a prawn cocktail as a starter. Dick slammed his hand on the table and said, 'Listen here son, you'll have tomato soup and a roll like the rest of us, and you'll enjoy it. You're at Carlisle United now, not Leeds United, so you better get used to it.' I felt about an inch tall when he'd finished and I wouldn't have been too unhappy had the ground opened up to swallow me. That was Dick's way of doing things, as many other players also discovered, but he was also a very fair and talented man. We went on to have some fantastic moments together, and it brings many a smile to my face when I think about my time with him at Brunton Park.

One dank winter's night we travelled down to Workington - not the nicest of places to play football, I can tell you - to play in a local derby. There was a joke doing the rounds in the dressing room that players had to be blindfolded on the trip down to West Cumbria, or they would never agree to go there, but that was all just part of the rivalry that was felt between the two sides. Both teams were near the top of Division 4 at the time and we were expecting a full house of close to 15,000 fans. As I say, the rivalry between the sides and the supporters was as fierce as anything I had encountered anywhere, so I wanted to make sure that I felt right ahead of the game. The pitch was rock hard, because of the frost, so I felt that it would be best if I tried out all of the boots that I had taken with me. After a few minutes of switching them around, I decided that none of them felt right, and I took myself off on a little jog in my training shoes. They were the old style basketball boot, the ones that covered the foot and the ankle, and they felt really comfortable. I wasn't slipping or sliding or losing my footing, so that was it, decision made.

Back in the dressing room Dick spotted that I was wearing them, and he came over to ask me what the heck I thought I was doing. I stuck to my guns, despite the fact that he was less than polite about the whole affair, and out I went for kick off with his opinions still ringing in my ears. After about half an hour I picked the ball up in midfield, moved forward, and let one fly from about 25 yards. It whipped in to the top corner, leaving the keeper with no chance, and it turned out to be the only goal of the game. We didn't go for wild celebrations or anything like that back then, so all I did was turn towards the dug out and throw a quick thumbs up towards Dick. He pointed at my trainers, smiled, and then gave me a thumbs up sign back. Walking off the pitch at the end of the game he patted me on the back and he said, 'Nice one Skip.' It may only be a small thing, but that meant a lot to me, and it was music to my ears to get praise from a man like him in a situation like that.

I think that incident completely broke the ice between us, and we started to understand each other a little bit more. I can honestly say that the man deserves legend status at the club, because the dedication he showed and the work he did were second to none. He was one of those rarities in the game in that he would probably have done the job for nothing, if he had to, and I guess that there were probably occasions when that is exactly what happened.

Mind you, I'm sure that would have changed if he'd caught us playing cards on one of our many long away trips. If there was a curfew, Dick would be like an old school master prowling the rooms and corridors and making sure that we were all in bed when it came to lights out. On more than occasion myself and Frank Large or George McVitie would find ourselves cowering behind the curtain in someone's room whilst Dick checked in to see that there were no wrong doings afoot. I actually think that he must have known what we were up to, and that he was just going through the motions, because there is no way that we'd have been able to pull the wool over his eyes for too long … there's just no way!

Another memory I have of him involves a photograph that was taken showing me and Tommy Passmoor lifting some kit in to the back of the team bus. Whenever anyone sees the picture they ask me if it was the first team kit that we were lugging around. That never fails to bring a smile to my face. It was actually Dick's pigeons, and he used to make us pull over and release them when we got to the top of Shap so that they could get some training in ahead of their races. Unbelievable, it really was, and I could never imagine Syd Owen or Les Cocker allowing it to happen over at Leeds. We were all used to it though, because the pigeons took pride of place in our shooting range. Come to think of it, heaven only knows how people like Frank Large and Ron Simpson didn't end up killing a few of them with the way that they used to smack the ball during our practices.

One of the most endearing traits that Dick had was his willingness and ability to make decisions. If something wasn't quite right, or if things were going off track a little bit, he would use his influence to sort it out. He would never undermine the authority of the manager, or go behind anyone's back, but he had this quiet, calm and strong manner that meant that he could be relied upon to steer the ship, if it was needed.

I also found that a harsh or stern word from him would be followed quite quickly by a normal conversation, on all kinds of subjects, just to make it clear that there were no hard feelings. I have much to thank him for, and I learned a lot from him, and I can say with hand on heart that he was respected by everyone at the club.

Down We Go

Unfortunately, things didn't really go to plan in my first season there, and it quickly got difficult for Ivor. I was pleased that I got my first goal for the club whilst he was still there – that was from the penalty spot in a 2-1 home defeat against Norhtampton – but there was a gloomy feeling that the writing was on the wall. Crowds were dwindling to below the 4000 mark, and I would have swapped that goal for two points any day.

The final straw came when we were knocked out of the FA Cup by a non-league side called Gravesend, and that proved to be too much for the board to accept. He was sacked shortly afterwards, and that was a very sad day for me on a personal level.

However, I don't think that Ivor had helped his own cause that much in the weeks leading up to his dismissal. We went down to Watford, and they had hammered us by 5-1, and we all just wanted to get on to the bus and lick our wounds. The directors were already in their seats as we climbed up the steps, and we heard one of them comment that we had played as badly as he had seen for a while. Ivor exploded almost immediately and rounded on him, in front of everyone. He shouted, 'Don't you dare pass judgement on my players, I will decide who has had a bad game and who hasn't!' There was a long, cold silence and I whispered to Terry Caldwell that Ivor had just made a huge mistake. I have no pleasure in saying that I turned out to be right.

We all gathered together to say goodbye to Ivor, and it was quite unusual because the newspaper had sent a man down to take a photograph of him as he left the ground for the last time. I have no idea why, but we all agreed to pose, so we were told to get together in a group just outside main reception. I then shook Ivor's hand as the picture was taken, with the rest of the lads in the background wishing him all the best. Looking back it's probably something that I wish we hadn't done, but it was important for us that we did get to see him before he left, so it was a small price to pay.

Our next manager was a man called Alan Ashman. He was a former player, who had resigned following knee trouble, and he was working on a poultry farm at the time for one of the directors at the club. He was also doing some coaching work for Penrith, a local league side, and we weren't too sure what to expect when they brought him in.

The thing that amazed me about Alan was that it quickly became apparent that his tactical awareness was non-existent. If a game was going badly, he didn't seem to have the ability to make the changes that would matter, and that could be very frustrating. Sometimes we would look to him for guidance, or in expectation of a change, and it wasn't forthcoming. That did cause some amount of consternation for a while, but we got used to it and we picked up some excellent results along the way, even though I have to say that it was more by luck than judgement in my opinion.

The one area that he did have an uncanny knack for finding success in, though, was discovering and bringing in really good players. I have no idea whether he had a scout, or whether it was something that he did himself, but he could find them at the drop of a hat. You just need to look at one of the first players he brought in to Brunton Park for proof of that – Hugh McIlmoyle. I mean, what a player and what an impact!

His team talks when he first took over were shockingly bad. Having said that, we all thought that it was just a temporary appointment at the time, so we weren't that worried about it. He would start the talks off, but then he would look at the likes of me and Sammy Taylor to take them on, and we would move in to confirm the jobs that individual players had to do, and then go on to explain how we should approach the game as a team. He was a nice man, a very friendly man, but I do think that he had plenty of luck on his side as he went through his career. Either that or he learned very quickly.

My first goal with him in charge was the winner against Shrewsbury up in Carlisle. All of the goals in the 2-1 victory came in the first half, and I can remember him telling everyone during the break that they had to get the ball to McConnell and Oliphant, because we had them worried. I looked across at Ollie and shrugged, because neither of us had done anything spectacular, and I kept half an ear on what he was saying as he went on to tell Hugh Neil to keep a close eye on their wide man, as if he knew exactly what he was on about.

The Carlisle dressing room used to call him 'Polo-Man.' He always carried a supply with him, particularly on a match day, and he used it as his way of telling you that you hadn't made it in to the first team. If you saw him approaching with the packet open, and thrust towards you, then you knew that he was about to tell you that you were on the bench for the game. Jimmy Blain was usually a victim of that, and he would always joke about what time the manager would be bringing him his consolation Polo. To be fair to Alan, he was one of the first managers to introduce the rotation system, so you could never really guess who would be playing and who wouldn't be from one week to the next. Whatever decisions he made, perhaps his own personal motto should have been – Keep them sweet with a Polo.

We couldn't turn things round on the pitch when he first got there, and a poor run of results meant that we were relegated at the end of the season. That was a bit of a shock for us, to be honest, because we knew that we were better than that. We had some good and experienced players right through the team; people like Reg Davies, Sammy Taylor and Les Dagger, and we were definitely better than our final placing would suggest. It had just been of those seasons where nothing would go for us, and we paid the worst kind of price for it in the end.

It has to be one of the worst feelings I have ever had, when it was finally confirmed that we were going down. Not only do you feel disappointed for yourself, but there is a horrible feeling in the pit of your stomach that you have let the fans down. You start to look at the games that were drawn, and you can pick out incidents in each one of them that, had it been done differently, it may just have changed the end result. You also look closely at some of the defeats, especially the ones against the teams that were also struggling along at the bottom of the table, and they are the ones that hurt most and cut deepest.

You also have to face up to the fact that it doesn't matter how many times you say that you were too good to go down, because the simple fact is that the league table doesn't lie. Peel it, boil it and dissect it as much as you want, you still have to start the following season at the lower level. That is really, really difficult to come to terms with, but you have to sort yourself out as quickly as you can, because the summer is soon over and it is time to get up and go again. That's when you can dig in and sort it out, because there is only one place that you can put things right, and that's out on the pitch.

The mention of Les Dagger reminds me of an incident with the Bradford PA player-manager, Jimmy Scoular. I had played against him when he was at Portsmouth and Newcastle, and he was an awesome footballer. His cross field passes, from right to left, left many a defence on their back foot as they were always inch perfect.

In this particular game, up in Carlisle, Les was playing at outside left and he latched on to a pass when he was clearly two or three yards offside. The linesman didn't bat an eyelid, and Les ran on to score with a great finish beyond the keeper. Jimmy Scoular was incensed, to say the least, and he ran all of 30 yards to have a go at the official. To the amusement of the crowd he grabbed the lineo's arm and hoisted it in the air, complete with flag, and shouted at him, 'That's how you let the Ref know when someone is offside you blind *******.' Our fans decided to boo at him so he turned towards them and started conducting them with his hands. To make matters worse, Les trotted past him and said, 'Read the paper tomorrow Jimmy, it'll show I scored.' I've never seen Les move as fast, because Jimmy was after him and I honestly think he'd have killed him if he'd caught him.

At one time during that season I was asked to drive a Vauxhall Viva on just a gallon of petrol for the Thalidomide Charity. People were given the opportunity to write in to the local paper and guess how many miles I would get before the car came to a halt. I told Mary that some old biddy from the paper wanted to take me for a meal at the plush County Hotel, so that she could explain in full what was going to happen, so I was given the full blessing of my wife to go ahead and do what I could for what was a very good cause. Well, the first surprise for me was the state of the 'old biddy' that met me at the hotel.

Not only was she very young, but she was very attractive, and it also turned out that she was going to accompany me on the trip. With it being in the paper, they sent a photographer, so you can imagine the look on my wife's face when she saw my photograph in the local rag, complete with the young lass on my arm, posing beside the car. She didn't say much, but one thing I do remember her coming out with was, 'Well, she doesn't look too bad for an old biddy, does she now Peter?' Whoops!

For the record, the Viva did 43 miles, 1318 yards, 1 foot and 11 inches … and no, it wasn't me who measured it!

A good friend of mine in that team was Terry Caldwell. He'd also moved to Brunton Park from Leeds, but he had one of the most amazing transfer stories I had ever heard. The chairman over at Elland Road, when they signed him, was a Mr Sam Bolton. Terry was playing for Huddersfield Reserves at the time, and Sam had been tipped off that the number 3 was well worth watching. Mr Bolton arrived at the game late and, on being handed the team sheet, read that the number 3 shirt was indeed being worn by Terry Caldwell on that day. However, Huddersfield had made a late change, replacing Terry with a player called Ray Wilson, who was having a run out as he recovered from injury. With the team sheets already printed, the change was notified by word of mouth – obviously Mr Bolton had missed that. So, he settled himself down in his seat and watched Huddersfield play some wonderful football, with the number 3 in particular playing out of his skin. The following Monday, Mr Bolton made the necessary phone calls to Huddersfield and arranged to sign the number 3, as shown in the programme, Terry Caldwell. The deal was done, and Terry moved to Leeds shortly afterwards without anyone on their staff ever having seen him play! Poor old Terry made his debut the following Saturday, against Spurs, and he was up against a Welsh international called Cliff Jones. I don't think he got near the ball all afternoon, and we got hammered 5-0. Terry quickly moved on to Carlisle after that, and it's safe to say that he turned in to one of the best signings the club had ever made, and he was able to put the Leeds nightmare well and truly behind him.

We always used to call him TC in the dressing room, and it was no secret that he loved a bet. He would run a book on many match days, so that the lads could have a flutter, and I believe one of his first jobs, after he retired, was actually working in a bookies shop in Yorkshire. His fondness for racing led to him losing his TV at one point, and I know that his wife Ann was none too chuffed about that at all. He was a great lad though, and we had some fantastic times together. He was another who left Carlisle feeling more than a little bit bitter about the way he was treated towards the end of his time there, and we lost touch with each other after that. Every time I went back to Carlisle, after I'd retired, people would ask me if I'd seen or heard anything from TC, and I always had to admit that I hadn't. I knew that he lived near Wakefield, but I had more or less given up on seeing him again when my daughter somehow managed to track him down. She told him about my 70th birthday party, and it was a lovely surprise for me when he turned up at our cottage with a big smile on his face and a bag full of memories to talk about.

We were a very close group of players in that dressing room, and there was a gang of us that had some hotly contested card schools. There was Terry, of course, Allan Ross, George McVitie (who was coming through the ranks) and myself, and we were the original poker pack. We used to claim our spot on the bus, or in the hotel, and someone would always have a pack of cards to hand to help us pass the time as we travelled around the country.

I had moved to a house up at Belle Vue shortly after I signed, and that was very close to the Pioneer Foods factory that our Chairman, Andrew Jenkins, owned. Andrew was a fantastic person, as dedicated to the club as anyone I have met, and he was also a huge fan as well. He did me a real favour during my first summer at the club when he gave me a job as a delivery driver with one of his vans. I would complain about the amount of lifting and carrying that was involved, just to make my point, but he would dismiss that with his usual comment of, 'Yes, but Peter, just think how much stronger you'll be for next season. There'll be nobody who'll be able to handle you.'

He would make sure that whatever my route was for the day, the first drop off would be bacon and eggs, or something similar, at my own house before I got on my way. It may not seem like much but it was a fantastic gesture, as it was a wonderful supplement to my wages and something that Mary and I both really appreciated. He has never changed, and he still makes sure that I am looked after whenever I visit Brunton Park.

Pipped at the Post

The following season was a much better one for us, and there weren't many teams that could cope with us once we got ourselves going. We went up with Gillingham, and I think we knew from quite an early stage that we were in with a real chance.

Mind you, we were beaten quite comprehensively in our first away game when Tranmere ran riot in a 6-1 win. As with all big defeats, it stung a bit, and we thought it was going to be another of those seasons where we wouldn't be able to pick points up on the road, as we lost our next two away games to Exeter and Torquay.

We soon brushed that aside, and we announced our intentions in earnest when the fixture calendar pitted us against Hartlepools United twice in the space of a fortnight. We won 6-0 at their place, and 7-1 in Carlisle, and we could easily have reached double figures in both games if we had taken some of the other excellent chances that we created.

Hugh McImoyle was scoring for fun that year, and we had lads like Reg Davies, Frank Kirkup and Barry Brayton playing out of their skins. Joe Livingstone wasn't about to be overshadowed by Hughie either and he kept chipping in with a steady run of goals of his own.

We notched up some huge wins as we set our sights on winning the title, and it was great to see crowds of almost 11,000 come down to the ground almost every week – bearing in mind that it was Division 4.

We beat Southport in a home game towards the end of that season, and that was another memorable night for us all. We went in to the game with 96 League goals to our name, already a fantastic achievement, but we wanted to keep notching them up and take it through that magical 100 mark. Little did we know that we would do it that day! Johnny Evans got a couple, Joe Livingstone got one, Reg Davies bagged a penalty and I popped up with one of my own, and there is still some debate as to who it is that scored goal number 100, because of the way the records were done at the time. I am going to take the liberty of claiming it for myself – as I'm sure the rest of the lads did as well!

The race towards top spot was nip and tuck all the way, and we won four of our last five games to make sure that we would be involved in the shake up. We were eventually pipped at the finishing post by the Gills, on goal average, and when you consider that we scored twice as many goals as they did that season, it brings it home just how ridiculous that method of deciding league positions was.

Back to Back Promotions

The following 1964/65 season was, at the time, the best the club had ever enjoyed, and it still sits proudly up there amongst the great achievements at Brunton Park. When I think about the players that we had in the squad, it is little wonder that we did so well.

There was a superb full back who sat just behind me, called Hugh Neil, and we had an excellent understanding between the two of us. If he needed cover, I'd be there, and he was always on hand to back me up if we were moving forward or breaking things up in the middle of the park. Tragically he was later taken from us in a car crash, and that was a very sad day for everyone connected with the club.

We also had Tommy Passmoor, and he was a really composed footballer who never seemed to be hurried by anything. Tommy died in a works accident after he'd retired from the game and, yet again, I was completely knocked off my feet when I was told about that.

Before I go any further, I will tell you a story about Tommy that shows exactly what kind of man he was. We were playing Everton at home (February 1968) in a cup game, and they had some outstanding players on show. Joe Royle had put them ahead, but we had a little spell where we were attacking, and it looked like we might get a goal for ourselves.

The ground was packed, really busy, and the fans were getting quite excited as we took the game to our illustrious visitors. During one move, there was a surge of movement in the Paddock, and the rickety old wooden fence that separated the standing area from the pitch gave way. Suddenly there were people and falling bodies everywhere. There were lots of shouts and screams, and you could clearly see the fear and panic on some of the faces right at the front of the crowd. We had heard the stories from the games against the likes of Arsenal, where people had actually died in similar situations, and none of us wanted to see anything like that at Brunton Park again.

We all wanted to help, but there didn't see to be much that we could do … but I then saw Tommy pushing his way through some of those who were stumbling around at the front. There were some, who had managed to pick themselves up, and they were obviously trying their best to get clear, but Tommy was ignoring this as he seemed to have his eye on one particular area. He then bent down, and I was stunned when I saw him reappear with a tiny girl in his arms. The poor little thing was screaming, terrified, and I have absolutely no doubt that she would have been badly injured, or possibly worse, had Tommy Passmoor not reacted as quickly as he did. Even though he had exposed himself to danger because, make no mistake, it was not a nice situation at all, his only thought was for the little girl and for getting her out of there as quickly as he could.

We all congratulated him and asked him about it afterwards, but he brushed it off as if he'd just been to the shop for a pint of milk. I genuinely don't think that he understood the magnitude of his actions, but he was such an unassuming character that it wouldn't have affected him even if he had.

Tommy is another who could easily have cut it at a much higher level. It's easy to say things like that, because the contrary can never be proven, but I have no doubt that he had the ability to mix it at international level. Again, if he had been in the right team, at the right time, he would have been noticed. He was so fast and such a balanced footballer with it that it was untrue, and he was a real pleasure to watch and to play with.

Our wing half for our title winning exploits was Stan Harland, and he stood out in almost every game we played. After establishing himself with us at Brunton Park he moved on to Swindon, and I had a smile on my face the day I watched him walk on to the Wembley pitch to play Arsenal in the League Cup final. Stan was his usual efficient self, and I was delighted for him when Don Rogers scored their only goal and won them the game against what was a very, very strong Gunners side. Unfortunately we lost Stan to a heart attack a few years ago, and he is another who will always be missed.

The local media used to call us (Passmoor, Harland and myself) the 'Big Three' because we formed quite a formidable half back line when we played together. When we came up against Shrewsbury in the FA Cup in 1966 one of the reporters, I think it might have been Ivor Broadis, had worked out that it was the 70th time that we had played together in that role. Obviously they made a big thing of it in the paper, but all three of us said pretty much the same thing. There was no particular pattern or plan in the way that we played, we just made sure that all of our angles were always covered. If Stan wanted to get forward, either I or Tommy would hang back, just to make sure that we weren't caught on the break. We were able to switch things around like that, and it seemed to work really well, both for us and for the team.

We were also picked out for praise by the away fans, and there was one amazing game, when we played Bournemouth at Dean Court early in 1965, when the home fans were cheering us with every pass that we made. When we made it 4-0 they started to chant, 'WE WANT FIVE, WE WANT FIVE,' and we could see that the poor Bournemouth lads just wanted the Ref to blow the whistle and bring it to an end. Happy days indeed!

Mind you, it wasn't all plain sailing. I do think that there was a huge moment in the season for us, just before Christmas, when we travelled down to play Brentford. We were suffering from another annoying dip in our away form, but even we were shocked at how poor we were in this one. Frank Large had kept us in touch with a first half header, but they ripped us to shreds for the rest of the game and we were left with some very bruised egos and a 6-1 final result to ponder. There wasn't much said in the dressing room afterwards, but one thing that did impress me was the number of people who held their hands up and admitted their mistakes.

That result hurt, but I do think that it gave us the slap in the face that we needed. It was never really brought up much, but we only lost three or four more games all season and we became a really solid unit. I did briefly speak to Alan about it on the way back to Carlisle, but there was no way that we were ever going to be able to put a finger on what went wrong. It was better for us all if it was forgotten as quickly as possible, and the best way to do that was to bounce back out on the pitch. Thankfully that's exactly what we did.

22

Giving it Large

Up front in the team we had 'The Human Bulldozer,' Frank Large. He had been around the block a bit – I think he had more clubs than Tiger Woods throughout his career – but he was a player who had a huge heart. The crowd loved him for that, because he gave us everything, and he was never one to hide away. We all knew the drill; if you had the ball, and you didn't have anywhere else to go, you simply hung it up and dropped it in to the box. Big Frank did the rest for you. Either the ball, the keeper, or both would end up in the back of the net, with Frank steaming through everything in his path to get the final touch on it.

Frank was from Leeds, and his wife and my wife got on really well together. Mary used to go round and visit, and there was one day that she was sat looking at the windows in the front room and she was trying to work out what was wrong. Eventually the penny dropped and she said, 'Aren't you going to put any curtains up?' Frank's missus said, 'Curtains, you're having a laugh aren't you? We're never at a bloody place long enough to get the windows measured up properly!' Like I say, he'd seen a few clubs had our Frank, let's not make any mistake about that.

He was one who would sail really close to the wind on so many occasions and he would take a chance every single time we went on an away trip. We would generally have some kind of team outing the night before a game, and it would usually be a visit to the cinema to see the latest film that was doing the rounds. Frank, Sammy Taylor and Reg Davies would sit two rows behind Dick Young, our chaperone and minder, and as soon as the lights went down they would be up and out of the auditorium. Two or three pints later they would sneak back in, and they'd be there for the head count as the lights went up with huge smiles on their faces, as if they'd been there all along.

Frank would stay over with us whenever we went back across to Leeds, and he would then drive me back to Carlisle in his Jag. Well, it was a beautiful car, we can't deny that, but he used to drive it as if he was Lewis Hamilton. I had to make sure I had a fair few pairs of clean underpants that were handy because I used to go through them regularly with him at the wheel. If we went via a route that would take me two hours, he would do it in 90 minutes just to prove a point. That was fine, it gave him the bragging rights, but it left me as a nervous wreck.

I can remember coming up a steep hill near Kendal once, and we went flying round this bend as if it didn't exist. Just as we came over the brow of the hill we spotted that there was a traffic jam, and a huge great line of vehicles were spread out in front of us. I nearly put my foot through the floor as I started pressing my imaginary brake pedal in the passenger footwell, and I was shouting at him to slow down. Somehow, he managed to get the thing to stop, but not before the bonnet had gone right under the back end of a big truck. I was sat there, nose to metal with a dirty number plate, with my life flashing before my eyes, and I could hardly talk because of the panic that was in my stomach. I managed to say something along the lines of, 'That was close, Frank,' and the stupidity of that gave us both the giggles. He said, 'It wasn't half, wasn't it,' … and then the silly idiot took his foot off the brake. As soon as he did that the bonnet of his car lifted up and wedged beneath the lorry. It was like listening to a car crusher at work. The whole of the front end was mangled, and he was absolutely gutted, bless him.

Another one was when he moved in to a house near us up at Belle Vue, in Carlisle. I should really have known better, but when he suggested that we take it in turns to drive in to work I agreed immediately, without thinking of the potential for disaster a ride in the car with him could be.

Anyway, it was his turn one week and we were going down Moorhouse Hill, past the Museum pub and down in to the dip, when the bonnet of his car popped up and flew off. There was no warning or anything like that, it was just whoooosh, and it was gone. It whipped over our heads, missing us by inches, and landed about twenty or thirty yards behind us. Thank heavens there was nobody following behind because it would have done them some serious injury. Not to give too much away but it's a safe bet to say that we were probably doing about 80 miles an hour as we set off down that hill, because that's how Frank liked to drive. I just sat there and shook my head at him as he grinned back at me with a ridiculous smile that covered most of his face.

Mentioning the Museum reminds me of many happy nights that we used to spend in there playing dominoes. Rules were quite strict in those days, and no women were allowed in what they called the Tap Room, so we used to be able to let our hair down and perhaps swear a bit as well, as we got on with our game. We made a lot of good friends during those sessions, and I somehow can't imagine today's slaves getting together for a 50p 'knock' in a local pub on a Sunday afternoon … no, I just don't think that would ever happen. Those meetings used to be particularly raucous if we'd won on the Saturday, and many of the fans used to come in to have a game with us and to talk about the match, because they knew that we'd all be in there.

That kind of interaction between the fans and the players was appreciated by everybody and it was one of the benefits of having the squad members living locally, rather than watch them disappear down the motorway almost as soon as the final whistle was blown. It is another aspect of the game that has changed drastically over the years, and it is now almost the norm for the lads to travel from all over the north to play for a club like Carlisle. I do think that's a shame, but they know no different and I suppose that we just have to accept that attitudes and expectations change, almost as much as the game itself changes, as time moves on.

23

A Pair of Jokers

Back to the team and the left wing berth was taken up by local lad Ronnie Simpson. He had a kick like a mule in his left boot, and he was a handy outlet for us to have. If he wasn't playing football he could usually be found on the golf course, working on getting his handicap down and his bunker shots up.

One of our playmakers was a tricky little footballer called Willie Carlin. He was built like Willie Carson, but once he had the ball he was almost impossible to catch. He was the kind who attracted the scouts, and there was little surprise when Brian Clough admitted that he was interested in him, and we then lost him to Derby County.

I can't forget our inside right, Johnny Evans. He was a real character, and he kept the dressing room laughing with his antics and his typical Scouse humour, but he was also one of the best players I have ever played with. He was as fit as a butchers' dog, and he would chase everything, even if it looked like a lost cause. He caused many a nightmare for opposition defenders because of that, and it also brought him more than his fair share of goals.

Willie and Johnny used to room together on our away trips, and they were the cause of all kinds of trouble with their wind ups and antics. My room mate for a trip to Reading was Frank Large, who didn't suffer fools lightly at all, and there was one night when he was pushed to boiling point by our resident jokers, despite the fact that they were actually innocent on this occasion.

We were in a hotel not far from Reading, who we were playing the following day (incidentally, I needed seven stitches in my leg after the match, because I had a huge gash in it from yet another 50:50

challenge … but that's another story) and Frank had left his shoes in the corridor for the porter to clean. Once he'd got himself ready he stuck his head outside the door to get them, and started ranting and swearing when he spotted that they weren't there. He immediately went along the corridor and banged on their door, demanding that they hand the shoes over immediately. The lads told him they had no idea what he was on about, but Frank was having none of it. He thumped the door harder, and gave them an ultimatum – shoes back, or else. Again, they told him to go away (it sounded like that anyway) and that left Frank with steam rising out of his ears.

The red mist descended and the next thing I saw was big Frank on the floor in their room, with splinters all around him, and the remains of the door hanging off the hinges. At almost that exact moment the porter came around the corner and walked up to Frank, handed him the missing items and said, 'Your shoes sir,' before he quickly headed off to get the hotel manager. We were asked to pack up and leave about twenty minutes later, and it took a while for all three of them to see the funny side.

As I hinted earlier, that weekend got even worse for me because I was targeted by a Reading player called Pat Terry once we got in to the game. We were exchanging views, so to speak, and the next thing I knew he'd come across me in what was quite a bad challenge. Dick Young got me to roll my sock down when he came to look at it, because we weren't too sure about how much damage had been done, and we were both quite shocked when we saw how deep the gash was. I needed seven stitches in the leg to hold it together, and I was quickly patched up and told to carry on. At the end of the game I shook hands with Pat, but I kept tight hold of him and pulled him towards me so that I could tell him that I was looking forward to seeing him back up at our place. He brushed me off, smirked at me and walked away, and that was that as far as he was concerned.

In the return game up at Brunton Park Terry Caldwell, who had seen the original incident, decided that it was time for a bit of revenge. He bided his time and then shielded the ball when he saw that this lad was running towards him. Well, talk about diving – I've never seen anything like it! Pat Terry hardly touched him, but TC went flying as if he'd been hit by a bus. The Ref didn't even speak to Pat, he just ran up to him and produced the red card. Terry Caldwell looked across at me with a smile on his face, and we both just stared at Pat as he complained at the officials and then made his way off the field.

Just before we leave the subject of Carlin and Evans, they had their turn with me when they dropped me well and truly in it on Valentines Day. A card arrived at my house, professing undying love and everlasting adoration and smelling as if it had come right out of a cheap perfume factory. Mary hit the roof, and wanted to know what I was up to, and she wouldn't listen to me when I told her that it was someone having a joke. The sniggers and the whispers soon revealed that it was them, so I dragged them up to my house and made them explain themselves before Mary chopped my head off – and possibly a few other bits and pieces besides.

I can also remember them taking the mickey out of me constantly when we played Chesterfield in a League Cup game, at Saltergate, during our title winning season. We were playing well, and I'd put us in front shortly after kick off, but they equalised almost straight away from the restart. We went behind to a really poor second goal, but it became a real uphill struggle ten minutes before half time when Allan Ross came out to claim a cross. A big lad called Mike Commons had gone up for it with him and, instead of heading the ball, he caught Rossy full in the face. They both went down right away, and poor Allan didn't know what day of the week it was, let alone that he was supposed to be playing football. With very few volunteers it fell to me to don the number 1 shirt, and I defy anyone to tell me that I stood any chance at all with their third!

Rossy came back on after half time, but he was very groggy so we stuck him out on the right wing, and if he did get a touch at any point during the rest of the game there was no chance that he would have remembered it, as he complained about a pounding headache all the way home. Carlin didn't play in that game, because of an injury, but that didn't stop him from teaming up with his sidekick to question my 'cat-like' abilities between the sticks.

They could be a real pain once they got going together, but we wouldn't have had it any other way as they were great fun to have around, as well as being talented and committed footballers.

A Night to Remember

All of the lads I have mentioned contributed enormously to our history making title winning campaign in Division 3. I know that I have spoken about many proud moments already, but by far and away the proudest of all of my football exploits was this achievement with Carlisle. It was made all the more special for everyone, fans and players alike, because it went all the way down to the wire and the Tuesday night visit of Mansfield was one of the most important games I have ever played in.

We went in to it knowing that it was winner-takes-all, because The Stags and ourselves had been neck and neck for weeks, so it couldn't have been any tighter if we had wanted it to be.

It was made even more interesting because of the fact that we had played Mansfield at their place just a few days earlier, and they had beaten us 2-0. I was furious about that, it could have been a costly loss after all, and it is one of the few matches that I have travelled home from in complete silence. Mary didn't need to ask what the score was when I walked through the door; my face told the whole story. It was a game that we could and should have won, and I knew that we'd made things that much harder for ourselves by losing it. Poor Mary did what she always did in these situations, and sat and listened patiently to my ranting and raving, but she drew the line when I asked her to come to the return game the following Tuesday. With the mood I was in she convinced herself that I'd blame her if we lost, so she decided to steer well clear.

Going in to the game the picture at the top of the table was a messy one. We were in poll position, with Mansfield tight in behind us in second place but, crucially, they also had a game in hand. Hull City and Bristol City were then giving chase right on our coat tails, so we just couldn't afford to lose.

Full time – 19 April 1964/1965	Pld	Home					Away					Overall					Pts
		W	D	L	F	A	W	D	L	F	A	W	D	L	F	A	
1 **Carlisle United**	45	13	5	4	43	24	11	5	7	30	29	24	10	11	73	53	58
2 Mansfield Town	44	17	4	2	61	23	6	7	8	31	33	23	11	10	92	56	57
3 Hull City	45	13	6	3	49	24	9	6	8	40	32	22	12	11	89	56	56
4 Bristol City	44	12	6	3	48	18	10	5	8	39	37	22	11	11	87	55	55
5 Gillingham	44	16	5	1	44	10	7	4	11	25	36	23	9	12	69	46	55

We'd actually played Hull just a few weeks earlier at Brunton Park, and the game had been the cause of quite a lot of controversy. Flowing from end to end it could have gone either way, and I seem to remember that I gave away a free kick when there must have been less than a minute left to play. Hull tried to take the set piece quickly and cleverly, passing it to their wide man instead of floating it in to the box, and that caught us all a little bit unawares. A lad called Chris Chilton took it to the bye line and then crossed it beyond Terry Caldwell for Ken Wagstaff to volley in. As they celebrated I went straight over to the linesman, because the ball had clearly gone behind before the wind had blown it back in to play. Fortunately he had his flag in the air and the referee disallowed the goal, because that would have been a horrible way to have lost the game and it would also have given Hull two more points, which we wanted to avoid for obvious reasons. Things were nervy enough without us handing our closest rivals any kind of advantage. It was double relief for me because I'd actually shouted at Joe Dean, our keeper, and told him to leave it, because I was convinced it was going to be our goal kick. I can only imagine what Joe and the rest of the lads would have said if the goal had been given! The newspapers the next day were full of reports on that incident, as well as comments on the fact that the club had taken record gate receipts from the 17,174 fans who had turned up to watch what was easily the game of the day in the Division.

It was also one of the few occasions when an inside forward had stuck to me like glue, instead of getting on with his real job. His name was Ray Henderson, and he took me by surprise with the way he approached the game. He must have been told to stop me from getting on the ball, because every time I turned round he was there. Normally it would have been my job to police him, but he turned the tables on me in that match. After the final whistle had gone, we made our way up the tunnel and I realised that Ray was just behind me. I turned round, put my hand on his shoulder and said, 'Here, Ray, make sure you turn right when I turn left at the top of this or you'll end up in our dressing room.' It really was that bad!

They did the same to Ronnie Simpson, because I think both teams knew that he was a potential match winner, and it meant that Ronnie barely got a kick all game. It was frustrating, but when teams use that kind of tactic against you there's nothing much that you can do other than keep going and hope that the breaks will come.

As I say, the title was up for grabs going in to the last game; winner takes all; a time for heroes and all that type of thing. For those of you who remember the Roy of the Rovers cartoon strip, it was like one of the end of season stories that he used to get himself involved in; one of those that as you were watching the situation unfold you'd be thinking to yourself, 'Yeah, like that would ever happen in real life!'

I think every player suffers from a few nerves before any game, particularly if it's a big game but, despite a few butterflies, I can honestly say that I felt extremely confident during the build up to this one. We were a good team, we knew we were a good team, and we felt really aggrieved at the way we'd let Mansfield away with it down at their place. It was time to put things right and give the fans what they deserved. There was a lot of chatter and bravado in the dressing room before the match, and we could already hear the fans chanting 'UNITED, UNITED' as we were getting changed, so it was one of those occasions when the sound of the crowd made the hairs stand up on the back of your neck. My last words before we opened the door and made our way to the tunnel were something like, 'Don't leave this to chance lads, a draw might not be good enough, let's go out there and do it.'

The noise when we ran out on to the pitch was incredible. The place was jammed to the rafters, with thousands locked out, and you could barely hear yourself think. The twelfth man did their job, because Mansfield just couldn't get started, and the lift that the singing and roaring gave us drove us forward from the moment the Referee blew his whistle.

We killed the game very quickly, storming to a three goal lead within the first twenty minutes, and we could see that they had given it up. The scenes at full time were fantastic. We had to fight our way off the pitch because of the number of supporters who wanted to get to us, and I don't think I've ever been hugged as much in my life. The most satisfying thing about it all was that we'd worked hard over the course of the season and we deserved it, but we also knew that we were making history. The club was going up in to Division 2 for the first time in its 60-year Football League existence, and it felt wonderful to be a part of that. To also be club captain through it all, well, it made me feel extremely proud.

Full time after the Mansfield home game	Pld	Home					Away					Overall					Pts
		W	D	L	F	A	W	D	L	F	A	W	D	L	F	A	
1 **Carlisle United**	46	14	5	4	46	24	11	5	7	30	29	25	10	11	76	53	60
2 Bristol City	45	13	6	3	51	18	10	5	8	39	37	23	11	11	90	55	57
3 Mansfield Town	45	17	4	2	61	23	6	7	9	31	36	23	11	11	92	59	57
4 Hull City	45	13	6	3	49	24	9	6	8	40	32	22	12	11	89	56	56
5 Gillingham	44	16	5	1	44	10	7	4	11	25	36	23	9	12	69	46	55

We were eventually able to get up in to the director's box, and the scenes as we looked down on to the pitch, with a sea of smiling faces beaming back at us, will live with us forever. We could hear a few people shouting at us to throw our shirts in to the crowd, and that soon spread so, one by one, we took them off and launched them in to the melee. Believe it or not I was approached by a young lad just a few years ago, when I was visiting Brunton Park, who stopped me in the car park to tell me that his dad had been the one who caught my shirt on that night. Things like that may seem insignificant, but it puffed me up with pride again, to think that a father had passed that on to his son and that it meant something to both of them. It makes you realise just how much the things you achieve means to people, and that can be very humbling indeed.

In amongst all of our celebrations on that night, and just behind the scenes, was the disappointment that the players and staff from Mansfield were feeling. Results meant that they had been pipped at the post by Bristol City. There were no play-offs in those days so, within the space of 90 minutes, they had gone from title contenders to being completely shoved out of the reckoning. Mind you, had things gone the other way that day, it could just as easily have been us who were left to ponder on what might have been, so we have to be thankful for small mercies.

None of us wanted the fan celebrations to end, but we knew that there was champagne waiting for us in the dressing room, so we had one more cheer with the crowd and then made our way back down the stairs. The club chairman, Mr Sheffield, was waiting for us and he had a grin on his face that stretched from ear to ear. He produced a huge box of cigars from somewhere and even though most of us didn't smoke, we were all puffing away within minutes. A quick debate followed as to how it would be best for us to spend the rest of the evening, and we were all soon suited and booted and heading towards town. It was a fantastic night, it really was, as the whole of Carlisle seemed to be out and about, and the place was buzzing with excitement.

With things in full flow I started to make plans for kicking out time, and I gave Mary a ring to see if she was happy with me bringing the players back to our place to continue the party. She said yes, of course, and I knew there'd be sandwiches and all sorts on the go by the time we turned up. Just as I was about to hang up and get back to the group, she brought me crashing right back down to earth when she said, 'How's your mam?' My stomach did about three somersaults as it began to sink in that I had completely forgotten about her. There was no way that she was going to miss the game, so I'd got her a ticket and made sure she was in the ground, but that was the last I'd seen of her.

In all of the excitement I had clean forgotten that she was even there. I remember staying silent for a while, and I will even admit to a slight feeling of rising panic, until Mary decided that she'd had her fun and she confessed that mum was actually fine and that she was sat in the front room with a big smile on her face. Good old Dick Young had realised what was going on as soon as I started on the champagne after the game, and he took it upon himself to make sure that she got home safely whilst leaving me to make a fool of myself. Believe it or not I didn't drink during my playing days, but there are odd occasions when that takes a back seat and you just have to join in. Winning the title, I'm sure you'll agree, falls securely in to that category.

The first telegram of congratulations that I received arrived early the next day. The last thing I wanted to be doing was answering the door the morning after a night like that, but I soon perked up when I saw who it was from. It simply said – McConnell = Carlisle United Football Club = Congratulations and well done – and it was signed by Don Revie. That meant a lot to me, and I thought that it was a great gesture from him.

Column Inches

I was asked to write a piece for the The Journal on the Friday after the Mansfield game, and this is what I had to say:

A lot of people seem surprised that we have done this well in our first season back in the Third. But I have sensed all along that the team has been capable of going up.

Early in the season I weighed up the sides that were tipped to do well, and I have never had a great deal of worry. People worried because we weren't always right up there at the top – but we were handily placed all along, and when we took those four points off Workington over the Christmas holidays, then that was it. I knew we were on the run-in.

This season's performance by United has essentially been a team job. They're a fabulous bunch of lads; always leg pulling.

The lads are deadly at this sort of thing. Stan Harland, with his sallow complexion, was asked this weekend if he was going home to Vietnam for the summer. Hughie McIlmoyle, when he was here, was always referred to as his 'Number One Son' because of his oriental looking eyes.

Willie Carlin and Johnny Evans, the titchiest inside pair in the Third Division, are known as Fudge and Speck, the footballing gnomes.

But this is all just part of the relaxed atmosphere and the companionship in the dressing room. The players have done really well as a group.

But this is all just part of the relaxed atmosphere and the companionship in the dressing room. The players have done really well as a group.

I think the team performance was even greater this season than last, because last time we relied quite a lot for the goals on Hughie McIlmoyle. This time we have got the goals from all around the team – even the full backs have been finding the net.

I have been asked when I knew that we were going up. It was when we won at QPR – and then we were faced with three games at home. I said to myself, this is it. We can make it to the Second.

It was a vital time to get to the top, with the three home games to go against Reading, Exeter and Shrewsbury. We lost to Reading, as it happened, but we soon made up for that with some very good results.

We had tactical talks and in discussion with the boss we agreed with his estimate of 60 points for promotion. He has had that figure in mind all season.

We have had a terrific run away from home. You saw us on Tuesday night against Mansfield. Well, we've played like that away from home all along. The Brunton Park crowd haven't really seen us do it, but we have produced this strong stuff away from home ever since the season started.

The thing about playing away is that mistakes don't matter. Someone can make a boob, and it doesn't dwell on his mind. At home, a player thinks to himself that he can't afford to slip up, in front of his home crowd. However, it's a sign of a good side when it can win away from home consistently. It means that your players aren't just 'homers.'

And when did I know that we were going to go up as Champions – that was at Mansfield a few days ago when we were beaten 2-0. It's a funny thing to say, but it's true. We went in to that game a little bit apprehensive about the fact that they were scoring so many goals at home, but the end result was not a fair reflection on the game. I thought we out-played them in every department, and even though they had beaten us, my worries were gone. I knew that we could beat them at Brunton Park on Tuesday night – and I was right.

We took them apart, and a lot of the credit must go to Jimmy Blain. He had a great game, and he had his full back on toast. It was just a continuation of Monday for him, for he did the same thing at Mansfield.

Humble didn't know which way Jimmy was going, and for this I think their left half, Morris, was partly to blame, for he gave Humble no cover at all. In our team, we all cover and cross-cover for each other.

Now for the $64,000 question – how well will we do in the Second Division?

For that, let's go back a bit. Let's go back to this time last season. I thought then that we would just nicely hold our own in the Third. I was very wrong – we did a lot better.

It's hard to say, really, but I've no qualms. I have played in the Second Division for Leeds United, and I have always thought that Third Division football was a lot harder.

Second Division football is more skilful. There's less hoof and boot about it, and this is what gives me confidence, for Carlisle are a footballing side with bags of ability.

We have come up on football. The sides that have given us most trouble have been the cloggers. We've had most bother from Gillingham, Barnsley, Brentford, and Shrewsbury, the sides that dig in a bit.

The Third is the hardest Division to get out of, and I hope we never find ourselves back there. I'm confident that we won't.

We are a young team, nicely blended. The lads probably haven't even reached their peak yet, individually. After a season like this there's no saying what the renewed confidence will do for a man. I think we're going places.

Tuesday night's chants from the crowd were amazing. It gave us a real lift. You've no idea what difference noise like that makes to a team. I was sorry for Mansfield. They were just like Christians being flung in to the arena.

But finally, looking back over the whole season, I think the outstanding event was the manager's decision to let McIlmoyle go to Wolves. Hughie was the hero, and Alan Ashman was taking a cool and very calculated gamble in letting him go. It paid off. If it hadn't, then the boss stood to be crucified.

What has happened here is one of the proudest moments of my football life, and I must say that I never dreamed that it could happen to me. I'm looking forward to a restful close season – to let my cuts and bruises heal up – and then it's on for the Second!

Article appeared in The Journal Friday April 23 1965.

Arnie Howe was one of the local reporters who covered the game for the paper on the Tuesday night, and he said afterwards, 'There are very few teams who could have lived with the sustained roasting that Carlisle gave Mansfield in that opening 20 minutes. It must have been frightening for them, but it was breathtaking to watch for the home fans.'

'The first goal, scored after just 14 minutes, could have been filmed to show over and over at coaching classes. Skipper Peter McConnell and schemer Willie Carlin exchanged passes in midfield before Carlin pushed a perfect ball out to Jimmy Blain. He sent it over for Frank Large to leap up and nod it in off the upright.'

'The noise around the place was deafening after that, and Blain has to be credited for doing the damage for the second goal. Carlin sent him away again with a great pass, and Johnny Evans prodded home a very poor clearance by their defender John Gill.'

'An even worse mistake from Gill gifted Carlisle their third on 34 minutes, and it was game over from the moment it went in. Terry Caldwell crossed a high ball and Gill completely missed it, when he should have got it away. Frank Large was taken by surprise, but he got his left boot to it and that was enough to send it trickling over the line.'

'I have to say, it was a wonderful night of football – real champagne soccer to go with the bubbly that was poured down the deserving throats not long after full time!'

Settling In

We settled well following the promotion, as I predicted that we would, because we were playing a really attractive passing game. We had so many footballers who could play the game on the ground that I just knew we would flourish when we were up against teams who would allow us a bit more time and space.

That turned out to be the case, and we showed many of the 'big reputation' sides exactly what we were about. The likes of Crystal Palace, Bolton and Manchester City all hinted that they saw us as a team to take points from, so we made sure that we proved all of our doubters wrong by getting the ball on the floor and doing what we did best – work hard, pass it and move, and make sure that we played the game the way we wanted to play it, rather than let ourselves be run ragged.

We kicked off the campaign with a 4-1 home win over Norwich, and Ronnie Simpson was the star of the show. Unfortunately it created a lot of false hope, and people allowed themselves to get a little bit carried away. Our weakness was our away form, and we only managed one win on our travels all season. We had to wait until April for that, when two Dave Wilson goals saw off the challenge of Middlesbrough, and it was a massive relief because there was a real concern that we weren't going to manage it at all.

I do also recall that it was my goal against Orient in April 1966 that all but confirmed their relegation. At the same time, had there been any chance that we were about to be dragged in to a fight for our lives ourselves, then that two points brought an end to that, and very pleased we were about it. None of us really believed that we'd go down, but football can be cruel, so we knew not to rest until the necessary points were in the bag.

Once more I found that Ivor Broadis, a former player-manager at the club, and now our chief sports reporter, was singing my praises in the paper. His headline on this occasion was 'So McConnell Does It Again' and, within the body of the report itself, he went on to say, 'Leave it to the skipper seems to be the Carlisle United maxim these days. It was Peter McConnell's foot that set the side on the winning road against Cardiff on Tuesday night and once again it was left to the United captain to bring a little warmth to a Siberian type evening. At Brunton Park last night, 8.41 by my watch, he virtually signalled the end of Orient's stay in the Second Division and gave United a further season's lease.' Whether or not that was the defining game for both teams that season is up for debate, but it was certainly an important victory, that much is definite.

As early as the January of that year, in fact, there were some of the papers who remained convinced that we were going to shoot ourselves in the foot and end up in the relegation places, but we kept defying the headlines and picking up the points that we needed to keep our heads above water. Sometimes we just couldn't win with the media, and the best example of that was when we dominated a home game against Portsmouth, at the turn of that year, from start to finish but we were still criticised for the way that we had played. What wasn't taken in to account was that the conditions were horrendous, and we also had Dave Wilson sent off when he lost his footing and clattered a man to the ground. It looked like an awful tackle, but it was actually all down to the fact that the pitch was like an ice rink. We won the game 2-1, with goals from myself and Stan Harland, so it was a bit of a shock to read the subsequent match reports that questioned whether we were good enough.

As I say, I thought that we were doing ok, and we pulled through that season to finish in a respectable lower mid-table spot. We continued to play football the way we wanted to, and we got ourselves in to the fifth-round of the League Cup during the 1966/67 season that followed, and that took quite a few of the pundits by surprise.

The two really enjoyable clashes for me during that run were when we came up against Southampton. They were a good side, a really strong bunch of lads, and we knew it would be tough with a mid-week journey down to their place. We were 2-1 up at half time, with goals from Chris Balderstone and Barry Hartle, and I said in the dressing room that we were playing well enough to go on and win it. Unfortunately Gordon Marsland broke his leg and we went down to ten men, and that made it even tougher for us, but we came away with a 3-3 draw thanks to another goal from Davey Wilson.

At our place we gave them a really torrid time, and Chris Balderstone scored twice to take us through to the next round and a match against Division 2 favourites Blackburn. The Saints home game was another extremely bruising encounter, with no holds barred, and our injury list afterwards was as long as a team sheet. Rossy was sidelined with a damaged shoulder when one of their strikers barged him to the ground, so Joe Dean had to step up, and Peter Garbutt had a bruised eye socket that Sonny Liston would have been proud of. I was sent off to the hospital for an x-ray on a suspected broken ankle, and it was a huge relief when they told me it was only a knock. However, I missed the trip to Norwich the following weekend and Ashman was left with no choice but to bring in quite a few of our younger Reserves. Brian Heslop was one of them, and at 19 years old he was a really promising player, but it was asking a lot to expect these youngsters to go to Carrow Road and get any kind of result. Unsurprisingly they lost by 2-0.

This is possibly as good a time as any to set the record straight about a goal that was credited to Dave Wilson when we beat Portsmouth by 2-1, at home, in January 1966. The fact that Davey was given that goal just about sums up the whole day, because it was a game that had everything, with penalty appeals and goal line clearances coming almost every time we went forward.

Barry Brayton completely lost his temper at one point when he beat their keeper with a lovely header, only for the full back to punch it over the bar for a corner. We could all see what had happened, and I'm convinced that the linesman must have seen it as well, but they waved us away and ignored the fact that the player had mud on his knuckles from where he had deflected it over.

Anyway, we kept plugging away and it was 1-1 with about two minutes left to go when Stan Harland beat his man and brought a parry out of the keeper with a fierce shot. I was in space, and my eyes lit up as I ran on to it and popped it in to the empty net. You can imagine my amazement when I listened to the reporters afterwards asking if they could speak to the match winner, Dave Wilson, because he hadn't been anywhere near the ball when I had scored! Unfortunately, it had already been passed down the wires, so Davey is officially named as the scorer of that goal in all of the papers and in the official records that accompany that fixture. But at least now you all know the truth!

The really big positive for me, from our first ever season at that level, apart from the fact that we held our own, was the arrival of our very own 'Sport Billy', Chris Balderstone, from Huddersfield. He was a very accomplished player who fitted in right away, and he was another who was an absolute pleasure to work with. When he was on his game he was untouchable and he would dictate the play with his passing and energy, if the opposition were daft enough to allow it. He was a player who played some of his best football whilst with Carlisle United, and he is a rightly still regarded as a Brunton Park hero.

So Close And Yet So Far

In Ashman's last season in charge we came within two or three wins of gaining promotion to Division 1, and people had finally stopped referring to us a little team from Cumbria. We were a force to be reckoned with in our own right, and we could beat anyone on our day.

Using that wonderful thing called hindsight again, of the eight points that were available from our games against the two sides that went up (Coventry City and Wolverhampton Wanderers) we managed to take only three. It's up for debate as to whether that was the reason that we missed out, but it didn't help our cause, let's put it that way.

Our home defeat against Wolves early in the season was particularly annoying, because we knew that they were one of the big boys. Whether they overawed us or not, I don't know, but we didn't get out of first gear and it was all but over when they took an early two goal lead.

The disappointment of missing out on what would have been a huge achievement aside, this was the season that a young man called George McVitie began to emerge as a serious contender. He had to be patient, stepping in whenever Barry Hartle or Eric Welsh were unavailable, but he soon gave Ashman plenty to think about as his pace and ability put the opposing defenders in all kinds of trouble. Add to that the fact that he could also score goals, and suddenly his young age didn't matter. He deservedly became an automatic first choice as we got in to the New Year of 1967, and he never really looked back after that.

I spent many an hour studying the league table in the summer months that followed that season, because it was heartbreaking to have got so close that we could almost touch the top flight. We'd have done well enough to stay up if we'd made it, I have no doubt about that, but it wasn't to be and we had to pick up and move on, and get ourselves ready to go again once the new pre-season came round.

For Alan Ashman, he had by now enjoyed a couple of very good seasons with the club and it came as no shock to us when bigger fish started asking questions about him. As I said earlier, the only real surprise to us what that he had managed to knit things together enough to make it all work in the first place. Having said that, he really was a nice, pleasant person, so I don't think anyone will begrudge him the success that he enjoyed.

One thing I will add about him is that there was a fantastic team spirit around the place whilst he was there. There were little things that caused us to bond, like in the February of 1965 when we were trundling along nicely at the top of the Division 3 table, and our next home game was against Peterborough. They were also in the top half, so we knew it was an important one, but Alan came in to the dressing room after one of the training sessions during the lead up to the game, and he told us that the ground staff were worried. The pitch wasn't holding up well in the weather at all; in fact it looked more like a ploughed field than a playing surface, and it seemed that the pitch forks and other usual methods just weren't working. Dick Young asked us what we thought, and within minutes we were all out there, pushing in divots and trampling on the worst areas to get it as flat as we could.

In the long run it probably didn't make much difference, but it was an example of the kind of feeling of togetherness that we had there at the time. I'm not sure if Alan alerted the media to it, or whether it was just coincidence, but a photographer was soon at the front door asking whether he could take a picture of us as we did our thing. The paper the next day had a big spread on it, and myself, David Oliphant, Frank Kirkup, Frank Large, Peter Garbutt and Joe Dean were all shown jumping up and down on the mud, with big smiles on our faces, as we did our best to make sure that the game would go ahead. It did, and I'm delighted to report that we won it by 2-1!

It Just Isn't Cricket!

Once Alan had moved on we found out that Tim Ward was coming in to the club and, yet again, we didn't really know what to make of it at all. He had been an excellent footballer with Derby, and it turned out that he was also a very good cricketer.

He inherited a side on a down turn, which was always going to be difficult, because many of us were edging towards the wrong side of 30, and I don't think he had a big enough personality to cope with a bunch of characters like that. He just didn't carry the authority, and I don't think he enjoyed the man management side of life at all.

There was one game at Brunton Park, against Blackpool, when we were 3-1 down by half time and we were playing like amateurs. I thought that we would be in for a real roasting when Tim got us in to the dressing room, because it just wasn't acceptable. You could have heard a pin drop as we all sat there waiting for him, because we knew that we had been way below par, and there were no excuses for it. All of the players were sat on the bench, in silence, and Dick Young was perched on the end of the row, just shaking his head and looking down at the floor in disgust. Eventually, after about 5 minutes, Tim appeared in the doorway. He had a look around the room, spotted Chris Balderstone in the corner, and it was as if he tip-toed over towards him, he was that quiet. Obviously we were all fascinated by this, and I couldn't take my eyes off him because I had no idea whether he was going to start shouting, or throwing things around, or what. When he got over to Chris he leaned forward, rested his hand on his shoulder and whispered in to his ear, 'Garfield Sobers has just knocked another century for the Windies.' With that, he turned on his heels and went back to his office. Well, Dick Young's face was a picture. He shot up, kicked the door closed and let rip with, 'CRICKET! CRICKET!

DON'T TALK TO ME ABOUT CRICKET. YOU LOT HAVE BEEN PATHETIC TODAY ...' If truth be known he ended up doing the manager's job for him, as had been the case on so many other occasions.

Another example of how easy going the new manager was came when we went on the long trip down to Cardiff. As per usual, Hugh McIlmoyle was struggling to stay awake whilst Tim Ward was doing his team talk and, by the time we had been through their expected formation, Hugh was completely gone. I waited for a pause, and then I stood up and asked Tim if he was going to do anything about it, because we were all more interested in Hugh's snoring than we were in the team talk. With Hugh being our superstar, everyone was quite scared of him, and that included our mild-mannered gaffer Mr Ward.

Tim saw him as a fans idol and I used to tell him that yes, that was the case, but he was also an idle 'so and so' who needed to be told what to do every now and then! I took it upon myself on this occasion, as captain, to sort things out, so I started shouting at the top of my voice. Hughie slowly came back in to the land of the living, and he was so relaxed about it all that he just looked at me, nodded, gave a little wave to the rest of the lads and then waited for me to finish so that he could go back to sleep.

When I spoke to him about it afterwards he just took it all in his stride and said, 'Aye, fair enough Skip,' as he promised not to do it again. I knew that he would though, and so did he. Whenever an incident like that cropped up Hugh would get himself back in to the good books with everyone immediately as, almost without fail, his reply would be to go out there and score a couple of goals to shut us all up.

One of the few occasions when Tim Ward was animated came early in his reign when we went to play Bolton Wanderers at their place. They had Francis Lee in their side, and it was rumoured in the papers that he was about to move to Manchester for anything up to £80,000, a big transfer fee back in those days. The game was an absolute cracker, and we went two up with goals from myself and Tommy Murray.

Wanderers soon pulled things back to all square, but we won a corner in the last ten minutes and Frank Sharp trotted over to take it. I'm not entirely certain what happened next, but I know that Peter Garbutt and Willie Carlin both got something on it before it eventually bounced over to me. I kept my eye on the ball and managed to avoid a couple of lunges as I volleyed it through the mess of bodies that was in front of me, to grab us the winner. We were all buzzing when we got back in to the dressing room, and Tim was there to slap us all on the back and congratulate us on what had been a very good win.

Just out of interest, the worst injury I have ever had the misfortune to witness took place whilst Tim was our manager. We were playing down in London, against Millwall, and Rossy threw the ball out to our new right back, Frank McCarron. Frank hadn't been playing much for us, but he was in for Hugh Neil as he struggled against a niggling injury that was keeping him out of the reckoning. Anyway, as the ball headed towards Frank I started to turn away, because there was absolutely no danger of him losing it. There was literally nobody anywhere near him. He had bags of time, so he went to stand on the ball to get it under control, and I think his intention then would have been to have a look around and decide what to do next. Somehow, he got it all wrong, and he went over the ball at a really awkward angle.

I was closest to him, and I could hear the crack as if it was a gunshot. It's the only time I've ever seen a break where the bone has come out of the skin and, I have to say, it's not something that I would ever queue up to see in a hurry again. Frank never really recovered from that, which is no real surprise because it was a horrible, nasty injury. Dick Young looked up as they were taking the poor lad off the pitch and he looked very sombre as he shook his head and mouthed, 'It's bad,' towards me.

We finished mid-table under Tim, but I think that was down to the quality of the players that he inherited rather than any kind of dynamic management. Hugh McIlmoyle came back in, of course, and he picked up where he'd left off, scoring in almost every game that he played.

The really frustrating thing for us this time round was the fact that we couldn't seem to kill off our home games. We drew something ridiculous like half of them, possibly more, and the number of leads that we threw away was almost unforgiveable.

A Cup of Joy

We had some memorable cup runs during my time at Brunton Park, and I remember running eventual FA Cup finalists Preston North End right to the wire in our sixth-round meeting at Deepdale. Sammy Taylor, our ex-Preston winger, rattled the crossbar with a downward header that I thought had the word goal written all over it. It skipped up off the surface and, instead of nestling in the back of the net, it came back off the woodwork and they were able to scramble it away. Shortly after that I struck a shot that rebounded off the inside of both posts, only to then fly straight in to Alan Kelly's hands, as he lay prone on the floor. They won the game by 1-0 in the end, and there was plenty of frustration in our dressing room afterwards at the way that things had panned out.

It was a similar situation for us in the 1967/68 season, when we drew Everton at home (this was the game I mentioned earlier, where the fence collapsed). They went on to play in the final, but they had a team that was packed with quality players. Joe Royle scored their first goal against us, and Mike Trebilcock wrapped it up just before full time. We had to hold our hands up and admit that we'd been outplayed in that game but, with most of that side going on to play for England in the 1966 World Cup, I think we can say it was fair enough.

My opponent that day was Alan Ball. It was an education to play against a player like that, because he had everything. Don't get me wrong, he didn't do anything fancy, or anything like that, he just seemed to get everywhere, and he never wasted a pass. They had Gordon West in goal, Ray Wilson at left back, Brian Labone at centre half and a lad called Brian Harris at left half. Their fans favourite was Alex Young, as graceful a footballer as you would ever see. He was another who made everything look easy, and he gave us a torrid time that day.

Finally, after what seemed like years of trying, we won a big cup game against Newcastle United at St James' Park. We knew it was going to be a big crowd and our pay and finance whiz kid, Hugh Neil, had it all worked out for us. Hugh was superb with things like that, because he could tally up your bonuses for any given situation and tell you to the exact penny what you were going to be paid that week. We were on crowd bonuses back in the 1960's, and it worked out that we earned an extra 50p each for every 1000 fans over 5000 that came to the game, and an extra pound for every thousand over 10,000.

As soon as we got to Newcastle Hugh had his pencil and notebook out, because our local papers had confirmed on the morning of the game that at least 10,000 Cumbrians were making the journey. We did our walk around the stadium, had a look at the place, and at 1.30pm the tannoy announcer came on to say that there were already 15,000 fans in the ground. Hugh did a bit of scribbling, then looked at us all and gave us a big thumbs up.

At 2.30pm it was announced that 35,000 fans were there, and Hugh nearly snapped his pencil in half in his frenzy to do the sums. A few moments before kick off they announced that there were 42,000 fans in the stadium to see the game. Hugh got us together in a team huddle and told us that we had all earned an extra £50, win, lose or draw, and that was before a ball had even been kicked in anger. Everyone thought we were having a final tactical talk, or a quick motivational speech, but we were actually talking about the nice little earner that we were on.

One of my neighbours from Green Lane, Tommy Murray, scored the winner in that game, and it was a victory that we all enjoyed. Some of the Newcastle players had been dismissive of us in the press, and they compounded that when they stormed off the pitch, without shaking hands, when the full time whistle was blown. I wasn't very impressed by that, as I felt it to be very unprofessional. One of the exceptions was big Wyn Davies. He was a fierce centre forward, with a fearsome reputation, but he made sure that he congratulated every one of us before he made his way back down the tunnel.

Another fond Cup memory that I have is from when we played Crystal Palace in 1966. The club decided that we would all go up to the Crown Hotel, as usual, for a pre-match meal and for a team talk. In fact, I seem to remember that it was a particularly nice meal that day, because we had decided that it was going to be no expense spared for what was quite a big game for us.

Their manager was the charismatic and flamboyant figure of Malcolm Allison, and that was enough to tempt my mother up to Carlisle to watch the game. For some reason she was late in getting to her seat, and she feared the worst when she heard a huge roar as she made her way up the stairs. She asked the person next to her what had happened as she started to sit down, only to be told, 'Peter McConnell has just scored for us.' I can only imagine how she reacted to that, but it won't have been pretty. The thing is, it was a 25-yard screamer as well, and I'd actually looked up to where I knew she was meant to be sitting and I had given her a wave as we made our way back towards the half way line. I thought she'd be sat there feeling really proud of her little boy – little did I know that she wasn't even there! We won the game 3-0, so at least she had the consolation of seeing us score another two goals.

As I have mentioned previously, Ivor Broadis was our regular match reporter then, and he always used to put a really big piece in the Sunday Sun about us. I was stunned when I bought the paper after that win because the headline that greeted me was 'Peter The Great.' Ivor decided that it was my influence throughout the 90 minutes that had taken us to our giant killing, and he wrote a wonderful article to go with it. Mind you, he didn't know how right he was when he said, 'From the moment when he seized on a Stephenson half-clearance … while latecomers were still seeking comfort on the terraces, the home skipper was United's inspiration.' Poor mum, she never forgave me for missing that goal.

The cup game that most Carlisle fans like to talk to me about is the one against Gateshead, where we were 3-1 down at half time. Lawrie McMenemy was their manager, and he had assembled himself a very good side. Amongst their ranks was a famous ex-Newcastle United left winger called Bobby Mitchell. He cut is in to shreds in the first half, and we were struggling to find a way to cope with his pace and movement. There were some harsh words said at half time, and that seemed to do the job because our striker suddenly woke up.

He terrorised them, turned the game on its head, and we won comfortably when he rounded off a perfect hat-trick with a header in to the top corner to make it 4-3. I am, of course, yet again talking about the one and only Hugh McIlmoyle. He was a stunning player, one of the best forwards I have ever played with and, in my opinion, he should have been selected for Scotland. If he had been at a more fashionable club, I'm actually convinced that he would have been. That's no disrespect to Carlisle United at all by saying that; it just seemed to be the way that it was.

Hugh had a bronze statue erected in his honour, outside the stadium, adjacent to Warwick Road. I have maintained all along that Hugh had me to thank for many of his goals, so I fully expect to see a statue of me go up on the opposite side of the road at some point in the very near future. It will show me crossing the ball, as I always used to, as I put it on a sixpence for Hughie to rifle in to the back of the net. Come on Mr Chairman, let's get it sorted! Seriously though, Hugh fully deserved that accolade, and he made it clear that it was as much for the players he had played with as it was for himself, which was very good of him. I used to room with Hugh for some of our away trips and he had a wicked sense of humour, and we passed many an hour telling stories and genuinely having a good laugh.

30

By George He's Got It

By now I had three children – two girls and a boy. My babysitters were a young ex-England schoolboy called George McVitie, and his wife to be, Ann. Our friendship started when we met at Carlisle, when George was a young apprentice, and they are possibly the nicest people I know.

What Ann doesn't realise is that George used to pay me to allow him to baby sit, just so he could get some time alone with his fiancée (that's not really true, Ann, but hopefully it will get him in to trouble anyway).

Going out in Carlisle with George is unbelievable. Everybody knows him, and they all want to sit and talk about football, or sometimes just say hello. George was always popular, and you could almost guarantee that he would be first on the team bus after a game. He always wanted to make sure that he had his place in the poker school and, with the speed that he got changed and outside, I don't think he ever missed out.

He was also in charge of refreshments for the rest of his poker school pals, and we never went short of travel sweets. There were always two full tins of them on hand at the start of every game, and he made sure that everyone got their fair share.

His nickname around the place was Scobie, after a famous jockey called Scobie Breasly, and he had heaps of ability out on the pitch. He was one of those players who could take on a full back and deliver an excellent cross, and all at pace. It was both a pleasure and an honour to have played with him, and to have watched him in action.

A few years ago they ran a competition in the local newspaper asking the fans to pick their best ever Carlisle United starting eleven. It was one of my proudest moments to read that myself, Hugh McIlmoyle, Stan Harland, Ivor Broadis and Ron Simpson featured in every team that was selected.

The only disappointment was that my chief babysitter and travel sweet supplier, George McVitie, wasn't included in the side. I found that to be strange, because he was fantastic for the club. He was the kind of player who would get the ball and relieve the pressure, and there were times that he would do things that would literally take your breath away.

One game I vividly remember him playing in was when he was just starting out, and we travelled down to Cardiff. Former Everton hard man Brian Harris was marking him, and he was showing absolutely no mercy at all. George was still finding his way in the game, so I had a quick word with Harris and asked him to pack it in. He just smiled at me and pushed me away – big mistake!

During the half time break I had a word with George and told him to make sure that he put a 50:50 ball between me and Harris at some point during the second half. Within a matter of minutes of the restart, the opportunity to do just that presented itself, and let's just say that me and Harris had a 'coming together.' There were no substitutions allowed in those days, so he spent the rest of the game hobbling around on the wing, and George left him on his backside a couple of times. Every time we meet up now, which is often, his first words are always, 'Hello Skip, remember that Cardiff game eh!'

31

A Sad End

My time with Carlisle ended sadly as far as I am concerned, and it is one of the few bad memories that I have from what was a wonderful period of my life. Things started to change for me when Bob Stokoe arrived, because I don't think we ever really saw eye to eye. I found him to be a very difficult man, who ruled by fear and intimidation, and he definitely didn't appreciate the problems that I was having with an Achilles heel injury that I was carrying.

Basically, about an hour before every game, I had to have my ankle strapped and an insert placed in my boot to take the discomfort away and to help me through the 90 minutes. I needed treatment every day, and I also needed a rest period, to allow it to recover, after every game. That meant that after a Saturday match, for example, I wouldn't then train with the first team until the Wednesday. This was tough for me, because I believed that a captain should lead by example, and you couldn't do that from the treatment table as far as I was concerned.

It kept appearing in the paper that Stokoe was offering to rest me, but I'm not really convinced that was ever a real option for me. My opinion was that we were playing well, and we had fielded an unchanged side for something like 16 games in a row, so I didn't want to upset that balance. When he did actually ask me about it, I would tell him that I would be alright for the match, and we always left it there. Nothing much was discussed at all.

Probably our biggest game of that season was the trip to Stamford Bridge to play Chelsea in the FA Cup. Dave Sexton was their manager at the time, and they weren't really playing that well. Peter Osgood had come back in to form during the Christmas period, though, and it was one that they were also keen to target to further boost their confidence. My ankle and foot were in a really bad way, because of the hard surfaces that we had been playing on, and it was probably the fact that I went all out to make sure that I played in that game that meant that I would go through the rest of the season in utter agony. As it was, Stokoe chose to leave me out anyway, giving Gordon Marsland the number 2 shirt. Chelsea played well on the day, and their quality shone through, but I was very disappointed not to be involved.

I battled through the remainder of the season like that, missing very few games along the way, because I knew that the summer months would allow me to get the rest and treatment I needed that would give me the best possible chance of getting myself fully fit and raring to go for the kick off in August.

Dick Young, a very good friend of mine by this time, had taken to ribbing me constantly about the amount of time that I was spending under treatment. When I went in to get my Achilles seen to he would go on about how he was getting a plaque put on the wall in recognition of the fact that it was now my personal recovery room.

He'd also dubbed me as Sir Laurence (after the on-screen legend Laurence Olivier), because out on the pitch I was winning us a fair share of free kicks and decisions due to my ability to hit the floor with a convincing jolt whenever I was tackled. To get my own back on Dick's mickey taking I would make sure that I went over at least twice in each game as far away from the dug out as I possibly could. Poor old Dick would come trotting over with all of his gear and, between deep puffs for breath, he would say, 'You better not be faking it again after I've run this far.' I'd look at him and wink and say, 'Of course I am Dick, but I've got us a free kick haven't I!'

Another part of the treatment that I was undergoing was a series of massages that Herbert Nicholson would do for me. I used to dread it. Herbert had been in the building trade for most of his life, and he had knotted hands that were as tough as old leather. After ten minutes with him you could hardly walk, and the pain from the pressure he applied was with you for three days.

At the same time as all of this, I had also opened negotiations with the directors to see if I could purchase the club house that I was living in. Mary was settled, the kids were in good, local schools and we felt like honorary Cumbrians with the way that people treated us. Talks regarding that were going extremely well, so I expected that it would just be a matter of time until we finally owned our own home.

The last thing that Mr Stokoe had said to me as we left for the summer break in 1969 was that I should work hard and look forward to starting again when we got back together. You can imagine my surprise then when, less than a fortnight later, I had a call from the club secretary telling me that the manager wanted me to go along to the ground so that he could speak to me. Initially I thought that it might be about the deal on my house, so I had no ill feelings at all as I made my way down there.

I should probably have realised that all wasn't as it seemed to be because, as I have said, we never really got on. Our first fall out had happened not long after he joined us, at a training session across at a place called the Sheepmount.

We used to go there whenever the ground was struggling under the weather conditions, and it was actually a useful facility to have, especially as it was just a short distance from the stadium. There were a host of football pitches and other training areas and a public race track for sprints and team relay races, and other things like that.

Anyway, we were all changed and outside waiting to start when Bob emerged in a fetching bobble hat and a brand new bright blue tracksuit. He looked, as they say, the business. He was another one of those coaches who could be a bit of a bully in training, and he could often be found literally kicking a player on the thighs or the backside if he felt that they weren't performing, so we took the opportunity to wind him up with a few whistles and cat-calls as he made his way towards us. He seemed to take it all in his stride, but that soon changed when he decided that he would run in front of me on his way to talk to the group.

I'm afraid I just couldn't resist it. I hung my boot out and he went down with a rather loud 'splat,' and then he slid on for another four or five feet through the mud and silt. Suddenly the beautiful bright blue tracksuit was a messy brown, and Bob was not happy about that at all. I set off running, because I could see in his face that he was out to get me, and I ended up being chased around the field for about 5 minutes with him screaming in my ear.

He was notorious for his shouting, was Mr Stokoe, and he would often come in to the dressing room at half time and really start ranting and raving. They talk about Ferguson throwing tea cups and the like, well that was nothing on what Bob could get up to. If it was within grasp, he would launch it, and he used to really rip in to players and make them feel small, even when they didn't necessarily deserve it. We would just sit and look at him whilst this was going on and, once we were used to it, I don't think it had any real effect on the team at all. It certainly didn't motivate us, as it is hard to respect someone who has completely lost their temper.

Mind you, as far as organising a team defensively goes, he was second to none. With us, he would make sure that Jimmy Blain and Ronnie Simpson were always back and giving cover and, at times, he almost had them playing as extra full backs. Hughie McIlmoyle would be left up front on his own, and if the ball actually got to him it was seen as a bonus. We were a team on the slide when he came in, so his philosophy was that we would get whatever points we could by defending the point that we had before the game had even kicked off.

A game that was typical of his preferred tactics was our 1-0 away win over at Sheffield United. He was using me as a full back, and my main job was to keep the defence in line, and I have to say that it was probably the easiest job I have ever had in my life. Wingers weren't being used much, maybe by the odd team or two, so I never really had anyone to mark. Our own wingers were playing as deep as they could, so it was very rare that anyone actually got through to take me on. I was almost playing a sweeper role, when I come to think about it.

Blain and Simpson must have been shattered by the end of the game, because Stokoe wanted them to do all of the hard work on the flanks, both defensively and going forward. Sheffield absolutely battered us throughout the match, but we camped in our own half and I think I cleared the ball off the line twice, with Jimmy Blain doing the same in the second half. That was the way Stokoe wanted to do things, though, so we just had to knuckle down and defend with our lives in almost every fixture that we played.

He was ruthless with his decision making, and loyalty and friendship meant very little to him at all, which brings me back to that horrible summer's day, when he summoned me to his office. I think the penny finally dropped that something serious was going on with the hesitant way that he asked me to sit down, once he'd called me in. I was shocked, but I can remember the next words to come out of his mouth as if it was just yesterday.

He said, 'The directors have decided that they want to give you a free transfer as a favour for the seven years of service that you have given to the club. So, you're now free to move on.' Once he'd finished he just looked at me, and I have no idea what it was that he expected me to do. I definitely wasn't about to thank him very much and wish him well for his summer holidays.

I could feel the anger rising, because I knew that what he was saying was absolute rubbish. I said to him, 'Come on Bob, you're the manager, you're the one who makes this kind of decision and I can't believe that you're hiding behind the directors whilst you do it.' He tried to assure me that it had been a decision made from above, but I didn't accept it, and I don't think that I ever will. I soon decided that I'd heard enough and that there was nothing left for me to say, so I got up and stormed out of the room.

I went straight to the boot room to collect my boots, and Dick Young was sat in there, staring at the wall. He didn't speak, because I suppose that he had to stay loyal to Stokoe, so I nodded at him and told him that I was off. He nodded back, and we looked at each other, but I don't think either of us had anything else to say that would have made the situation any better. I shook my head, he shook his, and I turned around and made my way down the corridor, all the while seething that I wasn't going to be able to say goodbye to some of the best people that I had ever met.

I was doubly gutted because I knew that all of the lads, even those who may have kept a little bit of distance, thought that I was a good captain. I gave that club and that job everything that I had from the day that I first arrived. I could coax, I could bollock, I could talk and I could cajole, and I know that everyone respected that. I loved the responsibility, and it was hard to be leaving all of that behind without so much as a thank you to the boys who had stood beside me for so long.

Also on my mind were concerns about Mary, the kids, our house, what I was going to do next, the fact that I had a really good relationship with the fans … there were all sorts of things going through my head. Mary, as usual, was the picture of calm. She listened to my story and shrugged her shoulders and said, 'Oh well, as one door closes another one opens. Something will come along.' I'll never forget that, because she simply wouldn't allow us to sink in to blind panic and start making silly decisions. I just wish Mr Stokoe could have been honest with me that day, because it would have made it all that much easier to accept.

I found out a few years later that he had done exactly the same to another long serving Carlisle United stalwart – Terry Caldwell. TC was due his testimonial, and he was a huge favourite with the supporters, but Mr Stokoe decided that it was time to show him the door before any of that went ahead. Terry felt extremely bitter about that and he refused to have anything to do with the club from that moment on. I find that to be a great shame, because I am sure the fans would like to see him more often than they do at the moment, just to say thank you for everything that he did whilst he was there. I fully understand where he is coming from with it all though, as it was a really bad way for it to end for him.

Time to Move On

Back to my own situation, and once I had cooled down I went back down to the ground and asked to see Stokoe once more. He explained that three clubs were already interested in me, and he told me to think about it and speak to them if I wanted to. The first club that I went to see was Gretna. I have to admit, I was very tempted by it, because the terms of the contract were very attractive. They offered me £500 to sign on, with a further £25 in appearance money per week. That was initially for me to sign on a part-time basis, which would have involved me in their training sessions for just two days of each week, followed by playing in the match on the Saturday. Eventually I decided that it was just too close to Carlisle, and I turned them down.

Workington, Barrow and Hull City then also asked to talk to me, but none of them appealed to either me or my wife, so I held out for a while in the hope that something else would come along. I think I've said a number of times, I have very few regrets, but one of the offers that did come in during those first few weeks was for me to move to Queen of the South as their player/manager. I think I probably dismissed it too quickly. At first the terms just didn't seem that attractive, so I wrote it off without really thinking about the long term implications.

The feeling of regret comes in to it with the fact that I'm sure that I would have made a very good manager. It was something that I wanted to do, and the offer from Queens would have given me the opportunity to learn the trade. I think I allowed my bitterness towards Bob Stokoe, and the fact that I wanted to get as far away from Carlisle as possible, to cloud my better judgement. I already had my coaching badge, gained from Lilleshall in the late 1950's, so I was more than qualified and, had I taken the job, then who knows where it would have led? I won't dwell on it too much, because it has been and gone and there is nothing that can be done to change it, but you will still find me wondering about how things could have been every now and then, especially when people ask me why I never took the plunge.

I resigned myself to waiting to see what would happen once more and as luck would have it, I received what was almost a perfect offer from Bradford City. My immediate thought was that the whole thing was fantastic, because it meant that Mary could move back to Leeds. When I looked in to it a bit further I realised that I already knew two of the coaches, Ken Oliver and Ray Wilson, and there were a few ex-Leeds players in the squad that were more than familiar faces.

The manager was a man called Jimmy Wheeler, one of the new breed, and he was very much in to stop watches, circuit training and track suits. This was good for me because, having turned 32, I found that my legs were starting to go, and the new fangled training methods were all to my benefit. In fact, there were often days when the younger lads would shout at me and tell me to slow down, such were my levels of enthusiasm.

When I think of how much training methods changed, even during my time in the game, it amazes me. When I first started the coaches would have one eye on their watch and the other on the car park. If the chairman pulled in it would suddenly become all shouting, flailing arms and activity, but that would soon die down again when he disappeared from view.

Our pre-match meal would be steak, salad and chips, and we thought nothing of stuffing ourselves just a few hours before kick off. Things were starting to change with all that as I came towards the end of my career, and it has moved on leaps and bounds since to get to where it is today. There are specialist keeper coaches now, strict diets and training programmes designed to hone every muscle in the body. They are good athletes these days, I will give them that, but with the money involved I'm not convinced they play the game with the same passion and desire that we had.

Back to Yorkshire

I accepted the move back to Yorkshire, and I soon found that I was enjoying myself once more. The only difficulty we had was getting ourselves moved in to our new home, so Don Revie stepped in yet again to help me out.

He invited me along to Elland Road to let me train with his squad whilst I got myself sorted out domestically, and that really did make things so much easier for me on so many levels. I didn't have to worry about rushing across to Bradford whilst Mary was up to her neck in unpacked boxes, and it gave us the time we needed to settle in and do things properly.

There was one day when I was put in to a team of Leeds Reserves, to play the first team, and it was an unbelievable experience. The side we were up against consisted of Sprake, Reaney, Cooper, Bremner, Charlton, Hunter, Lorimer, Clarke, Jones, Giles and Gray. It was breathtaking. Then, I had a look around at our team and we had players like Harvey, Madeley, Bates and Yorath, who were no mugs themselves, but we never got anywhere near them! I don't think I got a kick all game. The way they passed the ball and made space for each other was out of this world – and this was just a normal run out for them. It was a pleasure just to be on the same park as them.

I know that Norman Hunter had a reputation for being a player who would bite your legs if he could get near you, but the one that really scared me was Giles. He had the face of a choirboy, and it's fair to say that off the pitch he was as mild mannered as they come, but he was a terrier once he crossed that white line. He would leave his foot in and really put himself about, and I found him to be a very tough player.

The chairman at Bradford City was a larger than life character called Stafford Higgenbotham. He owned the Tebro Toy Factory in Bradford, and he threw everything in to his role down at the club. He loved mixing with the players, and he liked nothing more than to have a game of cards with us on the long away trips. To be fair, we enjoyed his company as well, and we had many good laughs when he was there.

I quickly built up a good friendship with a local lad called Bruce Bannister. If we had to work late, or meet up early, I would often stay over at his house, and we used the time to good effect, developing a system to make sure that the chairman always lost in our card games. It was a simple enough mechanism to employ, so we gave it a name so that the others would know what we were up to – it was called 'Cheating.'

Poor old Stafford didn't have a clue, and he would stare at his cards in disbelief as we beat his hands, often very good hands, every single time. The main game that we played was called Hearts, and the stakes involved were never that high, but our antics often left us giggling like schoolgirls as he got more and more frustrated at his run of 'bad luck.' The rules were simple – if you were caught with a Heart, it cost you the same number of points as the value of the card. So, a Two of Hearts would sting you for two points, for example. The really bad card, the one to avoid, was the Queen of Spades. That was a deduction of 13 points if you were left with that in your hand. Part of the game was the swapping of cards with your opponents, so if either myself or Bruce had the Queen, we would tap each other under the table, and pass it on so that we made sure the chairman would end up with it. We would go through the series of swaps, and all you would hear from Mr Higgenbotham was, 'Oh no, how's that happened, not again!'

Probably the biggest game I played in whilst I was there was a cup match against Tottenham Hotspur. We played well on the day, and earned a 2-2 draw, and we felt that we were unlucky not to win it in the end, especially with some of the chances that we had. Local lad John Hall hit the bar in the last minute of the game with most of us ready to celebrate, because it looked nailed on that he had just scored the winner as it flew towards the goal. Mr Higgenbotham threw a party for us that night, and all of the players and wives went along to his house to let their hair down. We crowded around his TV when Match of the Day came on, and I was left squirming as the highlights showed Jimmy Greaves dropping his shoulder and dumping me on to my backside as he raced past me to score the equaliser.

Other players of note in the Spurs team that day were Alan Gilzean, Martin Chivers, Alan Mullery and Pat Jennings. It was great for the fans that we did so well against a team like that, and everyone was looking forward to the replay at White Hart Lane. We played that one on the Wednesday night so, on the Monday morning, the chairman sent us all to a local tailor's shop to get measured up for brand new suits. We looked the part when we got to London but, unfortunately, that was as far as it went. Greavsie was on fire from the kick off, and his hat-trick was just part of the tale as they swept us away with a 5-0 victory.

It was also at Bradford that my interest in roses and willow pattern crockery was revealed to an unsuspecting world. A Journalist called Don Alred asked to speak to me as part of the build up to an away game at Macclesfield, and I gave him more than he bargained for when he asked me what it was that I did to pass the time when we went on the longer away journeys. Innocently I told him about the fact that I had 50 types of rose planted in my garden at Rose Cottage, in Oulton, and that I was always looking to add new varieties, and then I told him that I would often take a wander around antique shops and markets, wherever we were playing, to see if I could add to my collection of willow pattern crockery. The next thing I knew it was given a full page in the paper and I had to have my picture taken as I planted another type of rose in my front garden.

I enjoyed two good years with Bradford and, as my contract came towards an end, they offered me a player/coach role. One real positive memory from my time there was the fact that the manager, Jimmy Wheeler, had more idea about tactics and football than any other manager that I worked under apart from Don Revie, so I was tempted to take the gamble and work alongside him. I don't really know what it was that made me turn it down in the end, but something just didn't feel right, and I decided to look around for something else. That proved to be a very good decision on my part, because the manager and his backroom staff were all sacked shortly after I left.

In the mean time, Mary had taken a bar staff job at a motel near our cottage, and she was thoroughly enjoying it. She became very popular, and it wasn't long before the area managers from a nearby Whitbread Brewery started to enquire about who she was, as they were regular visitors to the establishment. Little did we know where that would lead.

34

Time Gentlemen Please

Mary had always fancied running her own pub, and her interest grew even more when she met and talked to a whole host of publicans and their wives at the annual LVA (Licensed Victuallers Association) meeting in Penrith, whilst I was club captain at Carlisle. She listened to what these people had to say, soaked up the stories of sun kissed exotic beaches and unlimited jewellery, and I think that planted a seed that would later grow in to us accepting our own pub.

In fact, that's definite, because the Whitbread men had rekindled her interest and she eventually agreed to talk to them, to see what they might say. She then arranged for two of them to come along to our cottage, so that they could speak to us both together. Now, our cottage was over 200 years old, so it had a very rustic feel to it, and I think that helped to sway the pair of them almost immediately. However, it almost went completely wrong when a man called Mr Owen asked me what I did for a living. I told him that I'd been a professional footballer for 20 years, and it seemed to stop him in his tracks. He took a deep breath and said, 'Look, Peter, there are three types of people we tend to steer clear of. They are ex-policemen, ex-rugby players and ex-footballers.' It was good that he was honest, but it did worry me.

Thankfully the rest of the interview went well, and they found that they were able to put their prejudices behind them, and we were offered an Olde Worlde type pub called The Angel. It had wonderful, old style beams across the ceiling and plenty of eye-catching brasses for decoration. The only down side of it all was that we had to sell the cottage and move in to The Angel lock, stock and barrel. We talked about it for a while, but I think we both knew that it was what we wanted, and we went for it. I attended a two week course at St Annes to learn about the bookwork, cellar work and administration side of things, and that was us ready to take it on.

We didn't change too much about the décor once we moved in there, but Mary soon got the kitchen going, with some help from her mother, and the reputation for good food started to spread. That in itself brought more custom, and we soon had ourselves a thriving little pub. Whitbreads kept an eye on us, and once they realised that the food side of things was taking off they moved the builders in and sorted us a brand new kitchen extension.

At the opening day for The Angel we managed to turn it in to a really special affair, because Don Revie came along to it, as did Norman Hunter and a couple of other former Leeds players, and the only downside was that Billy Bremner had some family business to take care of, and he couldn't make it. An ex-Welsh international called Harold Williams came along as well, and he was soon buzzing around and showing me what to do, particularly down in the cellar. He had also taken a pub in Leeds when he'd finished playing, so he had a wealth of knowledge about the trade that he was happy to share with me.

On the football side of things I had accepted a part-time contract to play for Scarborough, but I realised almost immediately that I'd made a mistake. The pub was by far the most important thing to us by now, and I found that it was taking over most of my free time. Colin Appleton was the team manager, a very good one as well, I have to say, and I decided that it was best for me to be honest with him. I asked to see him one day, about three months in to my contract there, and I told him that the situation wasn't fair on either of us. My mind was elsewhere, and I wasn't really giving him the effort that he deserved. He was excellent about the whole thing, he really was. He asked me what I wanted to do and we shook hands and said our goodbyes when I told him that it was probably better if I just called it a day.

I threw myself in to making The Angel a success and we stayed there for five years and, sadly, Mary's mum died just before we took post in our new place, The Hare and Hounds, which was a lovely little village pub in Rothwell.

Mary kept on with the home cooked food when we got there, and that soon became a huge hit, and we developed things on the social side with a football team, darts and dominoes teams, and regular karaoke evenings. Christmas and New Year's Eve celebrations were run like a military operation, with strict rules on admission, and people seemed to appreciate the way that we did things.

The pub became a massive part of our lives, and took up most of our time, but I decided it was time to retire from all of that after 20 years or so in the trade. The kids were all grown up and in good jobs and we felt that it was time to let someone else have a go. We started looking for a house and that all fell in to place nicely when a cottage in Oulton, two doors down from where we used to live, became available. Needless to say we snapped that up.

That kind of thing must run in the family because my brother Barry also tried his hand at running a pub. As luck would have it, it also happened to be my dad's local, and between them they built it in to a bit of a success story. They started up a football team and we used to have friendly games (if I can call them that) between our pub and his pub as part of the run up to the start of the season. Before long he also decided that we should have an inter-pub golf match, so I was happy to accommodate that as well. Now, Barry is a really good golfer, with what I can only describe as a unique swing, and he can drive the ball beautifully when he hits it right. Unfortunately for him our team won that one as well, so he had no hesitation in accusing us of being bandits. There was one hole, the short par four tenth at South Leeds Golf Course, where a lad called Steve Tranmer drove the ball from the tee straight on to the green. That caused a fair few grumbles and accusations of us being ringers, I can tell you!

One thing I will admit is that Barry is a much better singer than me. We both enjoy a stint with the microphone, but he has a lovely voice that can really hold a tune. There is one huge thing that I will always thank him for, and that is the way that he and his partner Barbara looked after my dear old mum. 'Our Dottie' was her name locally, and they took her everywhere, but they never seemed to begrudge a moment of it. It would have been very difficult for all of us if they hadn't done that, so our heartfelt thanks go to them for the way that they did that for her, and for us. She was a real character right to the end, even though her legs had gone, and she was a fiercely loyal Labour Party supporter. If people got on to her about politics she would tell them that she, and many like her, had stood up for them and that it was their duty to get down to the booths and put the X beside the name of the local Labour candidate. Anything else was tantamount to treason.

35

3G McConnell

Having decided to retire I then concentrated on the three G's – Golf, Grandkids and Gardening. I must admit, on the subject of grandkids, it seemed to take forever for our first one to come along, to my son James and his wife Helen. She was well worth the wait though and Grace is now following in the McConnell mould by playing for the Leeds United U16 ladies team as their goalkeeper.

It was whilst watching Grace train one evening, that it was brought home to me just how small this world can be. I had agreed to take her over to Tadcaster Albion, where the team were meeting, and I found it to be a thoroughly entertaining and educational experience as I watched their coach put them through their paces. The girls really went for it, and some of the things that they did, both fitness wise and with the ball, were way ahead of anything that I had ever done.

The following week I jumped at the chance when I was asked if I would like to take Grace again, because I wanted to see if they did the same things or if there was a different approach to the session. I have to say, it was fantastic, because the girls were given a completely new set of drills, and you could see the positive effect that had on them.

Whilst I was watching I saw two other men stood off to one side, so I walked over to them for a chat. They were also there to watch their granddaughters, so I mentioned that I thought the standard of the coaching was extremely high. One of them said: 'Yes, their coach is a lad called Ricky Passmoor, and apparently he's turned down a permanent job with Bolton Wanderers because he is enjoying himself at Leeds too much.'

I was almost knocked off my feet, and I said: 'That's an unusual name, Passmoor. I used to play over in Carlisle with a player called Tommy Passmoor.'

They confirmed, as I had begun to suspect, that Ricky was Tommy's son, and that was when I properly recognised him for who he was. As a boy, he had lived up in Belle Vue, in Carlisle, on the same street as us, and we would often see him playing and walking up and down the path, and I would also chat to him whenever I called for Tommy.

At the end of the coaching period I went over to him, and he told me that he had already realised who I was. It brought back so many memories, and we had a really good talk about his dad, and about our days in Carlisle. I congratulated him on the standard of his coaching, and I have to say that it was lovely to see him, especially having found out about the terrible works accident that had robbed us of Tommy a few years earlier.

It didn't end there, though, because I mentioned to Jason Tabor, the coach of my grandson's team (he, by the way, is another excellent coach who could easily make it in the professional game if he wanted to) that I had come across Ricky with the Leeds ladies and academy teams. It turned out that Ricky and Jason had coached together over in South Africa, and that they knew each other really well. Like I say, it's an unbelievably small world sometimes.

Grace was soon followed by Beth (a very keen netball player), David (a fisherman and a golfer after my own heart) and Olivia (the beautiful bouncing baby of the group), so James and his wife have their work cut out as they look after that lovely lot!

My younger daughter Catherine married former Castleford Rugby League player Tony Marchant and, after several miscarriages, they now have two wonderful sons called Rory and Leo, and we are waiting with baited breath to see what their interests will be. Again, they really are two fantastic kids, and it makes us so proud to see how well our own children are bringing their youngsters up.

My eldest daughter Debra has a boy, called William, and he has been football mad for years. I admire his bravery, because he is happy to admit, in front of me, that he is a Manchester United fan. Living in Leeds, that brings him plenty of stick from his mates at school, but he just shrugs it off and gets on with it. He loves training and has a good touch with both feet, so he is showing plenty of promise, and we all have our fingers crossed for him.

After 10 years of wonderful retirement my peace was shattered when Debra phoned me to ask if I was aware that my old pub, The Hare and Hounds, was shutting down. Debra and her partner Alan Butcher (Butch) had been working together at First Direct for years, and they both decided that they fancied a new challenge, so I told her that I would make some enquiries on her behalf. I spoke to Paul Shipley, the man who had taken the pub from me ten years earlier, and I found out that things had taken a down turn for him. He was keen to sell quickly, so we got Debra and Butch together with the leasing company and, after much thought and consideration, and some intricate negotiations, the pub was finally signed over to them.

At this point the whole family seemed to decide that they were going to make it work, and I almost lost count of the amount of people who wanted to help us get the place decorated and looking ship shape. My son James worked his socks off, along with his wife Helen. Debra and Butch matched them for effort and work rate every step of the way and Cath, my other daughter, roped all of her friends in to helping us out, and she seemed to bring someone different in every day. Her husband Tony also spent a lot of time with us, as did Dorothy and David (Helen's mum and dad). The list is endless, with our grandkids and many of our friends also pitching in whenever we needed some spare bodies around the place.

The hard work has more than paid off for us all now, with the pub open for business and building up its trade all the time. Mary is back in the kitchen and loving every minute of it, and it's great to see so many local people coming back to see what the pub is like, and then staying with us as regulars. I pitch in with a bit of glass collecting, serving and what have you, and Grace is also able to work for us on weekends, now that she is 16, collecting and washing glasses – and she has me as her minder whenever it gets too busy.

36

In the Strangest Places

We had a lovely moment in our pub not too long ago. The Rothwell team that I used to be involved with had arranged a charity match against some ex-Leeds United players, and I quite fancied going along to watch it. It was all for a young lad who lives locally who needed a new buggy to give him a little bit more freedom. I was at the pub with my grandson William, waiting for a lift, when Gary McAllister walked in and asked if he could use the toilet. I pointed the way and, once he'd got through the door, I turned to William and said, 'I'm sure that was Gary McAllister you know.'

He came back out and I confronted him, and it was then that he told me that he was looking for the Robin Hood football ground, because he was supposed to be playing in a charity match there. I gave William a wink and said, 'Well, it just so happens that I'm trying to get there myself, so if you give me a lift we could kill two birds with one stone.' As you can probably imagine, William was gobsmacked. The car was beautiful inside, a huge Mercedes 4x4, and he was really friendly with us all the way there. I told him that I used to play for Leeds and Carlisle United, and I mentioned that I was going up to Brunton Park the following week to watch the Swansea game. We left it at that, and I didn't really think any more of it, other than telling as many people who came in to the pub about it as I could.

So, a week later I was in Carlisle to watch the game, and I spotted Gary with his assistant, Steve Staunton. I wandered over to him at half time and I said to him, 'Don't suppose you can give me a lift back to Leeds can you?' He smiled at me and said, 'Are you following me or something – do I need to get the police involved here or what?' William is getting real mileage out of that one, telling his mates that he's had a lift off the Leeds United manager.

I also bumped in to Dennis Booth that night, the first team coach at Brunton Park, and a man who I had played against on a number of occasions. I remember Den as a full back with Charlton, and he clearly also remembered me because when he saw me he rolled the leg of his trousers up, pointed to a scar and then said, 'That was bloody you, that was.' Then he looked at my clothes and said, 'And you're still wearing the same suit you had on in the player's lounge that day as well!'

Recently we also enjoyed a bit of a reunion with the Robin Hood pub team that I used to manage. We had ourselves a very good side at one point, and one of the lads decided that we should have a get together, and it turned into an excellent night out. There must have been 30 or 40 people who turned up, at least, and there were many faces that I hadn't seen for a while. One of the ex-committee members had brought a collection of old photographs, so we were able to have a laugh at some of the celebration and trophy pictures that he had in amongst it all. I have to admit that I allowed myself a vodka or two, to the point where I had to leave my car in the car park and beg for a lift home at the end of the night.

The lads told me that some of the team talks I gave them used to make their hair stand on end. There was one big Yorkshire Cup clash where I thought we would be really tested, so I got them all together three days before the game and made a few suggestions. I asked them to think about what they were eating but, more importantly, to think about having a Saturday night off the alcohol. I knew that we would stand more of a chance if we were feeling rested on the Sunday morning, and I'm delighted to say that every single one of them took it on board and did what I asked.

We had a cracking little right winger playing for us, but there were times when he would disappear from the game and wait for something to come along, rather than make it happen for himself. Just before the game started I grabbed a handful of his shirt and said, 'You can make a difference if you want to, but you have to show me that you have the heart to do it. Now get out there and play for me!' He had a stormer, and we won the game 9-1. Some of those lads actually had trials with professional teams and, had they wanted to commit to it, I'm sure that a few of them would have made it.

The Bionic Man

In amongst all of that I had to have both of my knees replaced and I now sometimes feel like the bionic man. My first visitor following that operation was dear old Malcolm Lawton, a man I have now known for over 50 years. He'd actually phoned me when he heard that I was having the operation done, mostly to put my mind at rest. He'd had his knees replaced two years previously, and he took great pleasure in telling me that he had been bouncing around like a new born baby ever since. Obviously I was in all kinds of discomfort the day after my surgery, when he came to see me, and he just laughed at me and said, 'Come on Peter, I couldn't tell you the truth about it all now could I?'

Malcolm was responsible for trying to get the successful Leeds Youth team back together again so that we could swap stories and reminisce, and it was really good for us all when quite a few of them turned up. A lad called Joe Conroy was there, and it was great to see him again after so long. He had lived on the same street as me when I had first got married, and there was one night when his garage had been blown away by some really strong winds. When he walked in to the pub for the reunion I said, 'Hey Joe, good news, we've found your garage over in Middleton.' That was a rough estate when we were younger, about five minutes away from where he used to live, so that had him shaking his head at me, just like in the good old days.

I am now moving around better than I had been before the operation, but it has restricted the coaching that I do with my grandson's football team. That's frustrating because it's an absolute pleasure to train with the young lads, and watch as they develop, and it is credit to the parents that they show so much support for their boys, allowing them to play and train in what is often awful weather. Thankfully the new knees should mean that I'll be able to get back on the golf course, and

I expect an invitation from Ian, in Kendal, to be part of his team for the annual Carlisle United Golf Day – an event that I always enjoy.

And Finally ...

Putting this book together has brought back so many fantastic memories, and I hope you have enjoyed sharing some of them with me. Talking of memories, my mother died recently, at the age of 90, and my younger brother Barry found a box of memorabilia when he was sorting a few things out shortly afterwards. He gave that to my daughters and they pieced it together in a series of scrapbooks, and it has been wonderful to be able to look back on some of the things that we discovered.

It has also reminded me that I have had a wonderful life. Playing football was all I ever wanted to do, and I got to do it for some fantastic teams and with some fantastic people. With the amount of money around in the game today, people obviously ask me whether I would have preferred to be playing now, rather than scratching a living together back then, and my answer is always an emphatic no. I wouldn't swap the time I had for anything.

It was tough leaving home at 15 but, to coin a phrase, it made a man of me. National Service taught me self discipline, which was important, but the main thing was that I learned how to look busy, even when I wasn't, and it gave me a craving for jam doughnuts like you wouldn't believe. Being captain of a professional football team taught me responsibility and furnished me with people management skills that have served me well in every walk of life. I now know how to recognise and deal with the type of person who will respond to a rollocking, and those who need more of a fatherly approach.

I have done many things that I am proud of, and one that hasn't been mentioned yet, so I will now, if you'll indulge me, is the fact that I never once got sent off. How I got away with that I will never know, but it could have something to do with a little trick that I picked up very early on in my career. I would always make sure that I got a look at the Match Programme well before kick off and I went right to the page that told me the name of our Referee, and where he came from. Then, when he called us together for the toss, I would chat to him about where he'd come from and whether he'd had a good journey up or not. I also told him to let me know when any of our players stepped out of line, and I assured him that I would deal with it for him. I'm sure that softened their approach towards me because, without being too forthright, I was a dirty 'so and so' if the occasion needed it, but that was overlooked more times than I care to mention.

To any fans out there who would like to talk to me about anything, I would be happy to chat about the good old days whenever you see me, and I can also be contacted through the Media Department at Brunton Park if you would like to write to me with any of your own memories and thoughts.

To all of you youngsters who have the ambition, ability and desire to do well, just remember that you have to work hard to get the rewards. Listen to your coaches and play with a ball every spare moment you get. Football is the best game in the world, and it makes for a fantastic career, but you have to decide from the outset that you are going to give it everything. If you don't, it simply won't happen for you.

Thank you all for taking the time to reminisce with me … and here's to the next chapter in about 20 years time!

Peter McConnell

PS - Just as we were going to print with this book I received a call from Andrew Jenkins, the chairman of Carlisle United, and he gave me some fantastic news. It has been decided that a new bar, in the East Stand area of the ground, is to be named 'McConnell's Bar' in recognition of my services to the club. I would like to go on record and say just how proud I am to hear that this is happening, and I can't thank everyone at Brunton Park enough for what is a wonderful gesture. It is something that both I and my family really appreciate, and I am sure that it will be an emotional day when we officially declare it open for use. Once again, thank you for what is a fantastic gesture from a fantastic football club.

The McConnell
FACT-FILE

Position: Wing Half
Born: 3 March 1937, Reddish, England
Height: 175cm
Weight: 74kg

Managers:

Major Frank Buckley	Leeds United	June 1952 to April 1953
Raich Carter	Leeds United	May 1953 to June 1958
Bill Lambton	Leeds United	December 1958 to April 1959
Bob Roxburgh	Leeds United	Caretaker
Jack Taylor	Leeds United	May 1959 to March 1961
Don Revie	Leeds United	March 1961 to August 1962
Ivor Powell	Carlisle United	August 1962 to February 1963
Alan Ashman	Carlisle United	February 1963 to June 1967
Tim Ward	Carlisle United	September 1967 to September 1968
Bob Stokoe	Carlisle United	September 1968 to June 1969
Jimmy Wheeler	Bradford City	July 1969 to June 1971
Colin Appleton	Scarborough	June to September 1971

Consolidated Appearance Stats:

	League Apps	League Goals	FA Cup Apps	FA Cup Goals	League Cup Apps	League Cup Goals
Leeds United	48	4	2		3	1
Carlisle United	272 (1)	26	17	1	17	1
Bradford City	76 (3)	0	8	0	4	0
Scarborough	*No accurate details available*					

Leeds United Appearance Stats in Detail:

	League		FA Cup		League Cup		Europe		Other	
Season	**Apps**	**Goals**	**Apps**	**Goals**	**Apps**	**Goals**	**Apps**	**Goals**	**Apps**	**Goals**
1958 - 1959	6	0	0	0	0	0	0	0	0	0
1959 - 1960	8	0	0	0	0	0	0	0	0	0
1960 - 1961	11	1	0	0	0	0	0	0	0	0
1961 - 1962	23	3	2	0	3	1	0	0	0	0
Total	**48**	**4**	**2**	**0**	**3**	**1**	**0**	**0**	**0**	**0**

Carlisle United Appearance Stats in Detail:

Season	League		FA Cup		League Cup		Other	
	Apps	Goals	Apps	Goals	Apps	Goals	Apps	Goals
1962 - 1963	43	3	3	0	3	0	0	0
1963 - 1964	44	7	5	0	2	0	0	0
1964 - 1965	44	7	1	0	4	1	0	0
1965 - 1966	41	4	4	1	1	0	0	0
1966 - 1967	37 (1)	3	2	0	5	0	0	0
1967 - 1968	40	2	2	0	1	0	0	0
1968 - 1969	23	0	0	0	1	0	0	0
Total	272 (1)	26	17	1	17	1	0	0

Bradford City Appearance Stats in Detail:

Season	League		FA Cup		League Cup		Other	
	Apps	Goals	Apps	Goals	Apps	Goals	Apps	Goals
1969 - 1970	34 (2)	0	4	0	3	0	0	0
1970 - 1971	42 (1)	0	4	0	1	0	0	0
Total	76 (3)	0	8	0	4	0	0	0

Leeds United in the McConnell First Team Years:

Season 1958/59

Date	Opponents	Result	Crowd	Scorers
23/08/1958	Bolton Wanderers (A)	0 - 4	25922	-
26/08/1958	Luton Town (H)	1 - 1	25498	Crowe (pen)
30/08/1958	Burnley (H)	1 - 1	22739	Forrest
03/09/1958	Luton Town (A)	1 - 1	13497	Baird
06/09/1958	Preston North End (A)	2 - 1	22765	Overfield, Baird (pen)
10/09/1958	Birmingham City (H)	0 - 0	25228	-
13/09/1958	Leicester City (H)	1 - 1	23487	Meek
17/09/1958	Birmingham City (A)	1 - 4	24068	Forrest
20/09/1958	Everton (A)	2 - 3	31105	Cush, Crowe
27/09/1958	Arsenal (H)	2 - 1	33961	Overfield, Crowe (pen)
04/10/1958	Manchester City (A)	1 - 2	31989	OG
11/10/1958	Portsmouth (A)	0 - 2	22570	-
18/10/1958	Aston Villa (H)	0 - 0	21088	-
25/10/1958	Tottenham Hotspur (A)	3 - 2	38691	Cush, O'Brien, Overfield
01/11/1958	Manchester United (H)	1 - 2	48574	Shackleton
08/11/1958	Chelsea (A)	0 - 2	33357	-
15/11/1958	Blackpool (H)	1 - 1	29252	Crowe
22/11/1958	Blackburn Rovers (A)	4 - 2	28727	Humphries, Shackleton (3)
29/11/1958	Newcastle United (H)	3 - 2	32732	OG, Crowe, Overfield
06/12/1958	West Ham United (A)	3 - 2	22022	OG, Overfield, Crowe (pen)
13/12/1958	Nottingham Forest (H)	1 - 0	26341	Crowe
20/12/1958	Bolton Wanderers (H)	3 - 4	28534	Gibson, Shackleton, Crowe (pen)
26/12/1958	West Bromwich Albion (A)	2 - 1	34878	Humphries, Crowe (pen)
27/12/1958	West Bromwich Albion (H)	0 - 1	44929	-
03/01/1959	Burnley (A)	1 - 3	26013	Shackleton
10/01/1959	Luton Town (FACR3) (A)	1 - 5	18354	Shackleton
17/01/1959	Preston North End (H)	1 - 3	22043	Revie
31/01/1959	Leicester City (A)	1 - 0	23376	Shackleton

07/02/1959	Everton (H)	1 - 0	18200	Shackleton
14/02/1959	Wolverhampton Wanderers (A)	2 - 6	26790	Overfield, Shackleton
21/02/1959	Manchester City (H)	0 - 4	18515	-
24/02/1959	Arsenal (A)	0 - 1	30034	-
28/02/1959	Portsmouth (H)	1 - 1	14900	Cush
07/03/1959	Aston Villa (A)	1 - 2	27631	Overfield
14/03/1959	Tottenham Hotspur (H)	3 - 1	17010	Crowe, Overfield, Shackleton
21/03/1959	Manchester United (A)	0 - 4	45473	-
28/03/1959	Chelsea (H)	4 - 0	16676	Crowe, O'Brien (2), Shackleton
31/03/1959	Wolverhampton Wanderers (H)	1 - 3	35819	Crowe
04/04/1959	Blackpool (A)	0 - 3	14089	-
11/04/1959	Blackburn Rovers (H)	2 - 1	15232	Charlton, Shackleton
18/04/1959	Newcastle United (A)	2 - 2	19321	Revie, Peyton
22/04/1959	Nottingham Forest (A)	3 - 0	18650	Shackleton (3)
25/04/1959	West Ham United (H)	1 - 0	11257	Shackleton

Division 1 Final Standings 1958/59	Pld	Home					Away					Overall					Pts	GA
		W	D	L	F	A	W	D	L	F	A	W	D	L	F	A		
1 Wolverhampton Wanderers	42	15	3	3	68	19	13	2	6	42	30	28	5	9	110	49	61	2.24
2 Manchester United	42	14	4	3	58	27	10	3	8	45	39	24	7	11	103	66	55	1.56
3 Arsenal	42	14	3	4	53	29	7	5	9	35	39	21	8	13	88	68	50	1.29
4 Bolton Wanderers	42	14	3	4	56	30	6	7	8	23	36	20	10	12	79	66	50	1.20
5 West Bromwich Albion	42	8	7	6	41	33	10	6	5	47	35	18	13	11	88	68	49	1.29
6 West Ham United	42	15	3	3	59	29	6	3	12	26	41	21	6	15	85	70	48	1.21
7 Burnley	42	11	4	6	41	29	8	6	7	40	41	19	10	13	81	70	48	1.16
8 Blackpool	42	12	7	2	39	13	6	4	11	27	36	18	11	13	66	49	47	1.35
9 Birmingham City	42	14	1	6	54	35	6	5	10	30	33	20	6	16	84	68	46	1.24
10 Blackburn Rovers	42	12	3	6	48	28	5	7	9	28	42	17	10	15	76	70	44	1.09
11 Newcastle United	42	11	3	7	40	29	6	4	11	40	51	17	7	18	80	80	41	1.00
12 Preston North End	42	9	3	9	40	39	8	4	9	30	38	17	7	18	70	77	41	0.91
13 Nottingham Forest	42	9	4	8	37	32	8	2	11	34	42	17	6	19	71	74	40	0.96
14 Chelsea	42	13	2	6	52	37	5	2	14	25	61	18	4	20	77	98	40	0.79
15 Leeds United	**42**	**8**	**7**	**6**	**28**	**27**	**7**	**2**	**12**	**29**	**47**	**15**	**9**	**18**	**57**	**74**	**39**	**0.77**
16 Everton	42	11	3	7	39	38	6	1	14	32	49	17	4	21	71	87	38	0.82
17 Luton Town	42	11	6	4	50	26	1	7	13	18	45	12	13	17	68	71	37	0.96
18 Tottenham Hotspur	42	10	3	8	56	42	3	7	11	29	53	13	10	19	85	95	36	0.89
19 Leicester City	42	7	6	8	34	36	4	4	13	33	62	11	10	21	67	98	32	0.68
20 Manchester City	42	8	7	6	40	32	3	2	16	24	63	11	9	22	64	95	31	0.67
21 Aston Villa	42	8	5	8	31	33	3	3	15	27	54	11	8	23	58	87	30	0.67
22 Portsmouth	42	5	4	12	38	47	1	5	15	26	65	6	9	27	64	112	21	0.57

Season 1959/60

Date	Opponents	Result	Crowd	Scorers
22/08/1959	Burnley (H)	2 - 3	20233	Charlton, Cush (pen)
26/08/1959	Leicester City (A)	2 - 3	24790	Cush, Crowe
29/08/1959	Luton Town (A)	1 - 0	15822	Revie
02/09/1959	Leicester City (H)	1 - 1	18384	Crowe
05/09/1959	West Ham United (A)	2 - 1	27777	Crowe (2, 1 pen)
09/09/1959	Manchester United (A)	0 - 6	48619	-
12/09/1959	Chelsea (H)	2 - 1	17011	Crowe (2)
16/09/1959	Manchester United (H)	2 - 2	34048	Cush, Crowe
19/09/1959	West Bromwich Albion (A)	0 - 3	26364	-
26/09/1959	Newcastle United (H)	2 - 3	28306	Revie, McCole
03/10/1959	Birmingham City (A)	0 - 2	25301	-
10/10/1959	Everton (H)	3 - 3	19122	McCole, Francis, Crowe (pen)
17/10/1959	Blackpool (A)	3 - 3	22301	McCole (2), Francis
24/10/1959	Blackburn Rovers (H)	0 - 1	17159	-
31/10/1959	Bolton Wanderers (A)	1 - 1	20183	McCole
07/11/1959	Arsenal (H)	3 - 2	21617	McCole, Peyton (2)
14/11/1959	Wolverhampton Wanderers (A)	2 - 4	21546	Crowe, Peyton
21/11/1959	Sheffield Wednesday (H)	1 - 3	21260	McCole
28/11/1959	Nottingham Forest (A)	1 - 4	21366	Revie
05/12/1959	Fulham (H)	1 - 4	18846	McCole
12/12/1959	Manchester City (A)	3 - 3	19715	Crowe, Revie, Gibson
19/12/1959	Burnley (A)	1 - 0	17398	Overfield
26/12/1959	Tottenham Hotspur (H)	2 - 4	36037	McCole (2)
28/12/1959	Tottenham Hotspur (A)	4 - 1	54170	Meek, McCole (2) Cameron
02/01/1960	Luton Town (H)	1 - 1	19921	McCole
09/01/1960	Aston Villa (FACR3) (A)	1 - 2	43421	McCole
16/01/1960	West Ham United (H)	3 - 0	15284	Meek, Crowe, McCole
23/01/1960	Chelsea (A)	3 - 1	18963	McCole (2), Peyton
06/02/1960	West Bromwich Albion (H)	1 - 4	23729	McCole (pen)
13/02/1960	Newcastle United (A)	1 - 2	16148	Revie
27/02/1960	Fulham (A)	0 - 5	23355	-
05/03/1960	Blackpool (H)	2 - 4	23127	Meek, McCole
09/03/1960	Birmingham City (H)	3 - 3	8557	Revie (2), Bremner
19/03/1960	Manchester City (H)	4 - 3	32545	Peyton, Bremner, McCole (2 pens)
26/03/1960	Arsenal (A)	1 - 1	19597	Gibson
02/04/1960	Wolverhampton Wanderers (H)	0 - 3	29492	-

Date	Opponent	Score	Att.	Scorers
09/04/1960	Sheffield Wednesday (A)	0 - 1	27073	-
16/04/1960	Bolton Wanderers (H)	1 - 0	19272	Charlton
18/04/1960	Preston North End (A)	1 - 1	15879	Gibson
19/04/1960	Preston North End (H)	2 - 1	23764	Francis, Charlton
23/04/1960	Everton (A)	0 - 1	37885	-
27/04/1960	Blackburn Rovers (A)	2 - 3	19295	Meek, McCole
30/04/1960	Nottingham Forest (H)	1 - 0	11699	McCole (pen)

Division 1 Final Standings 1959/60	Pld	Home					Away					Overall					Pts	GA
		W	D	L	F	A	W	D	L	F	A	W	D	L	F	A		
1 Burnley	42	15	2	4	52	28	9	5	7	33	33	24	7	11	85	61	55	1.39
2 Wolverhampton Wanderers	42	15	3	3	63	28	9	3	9	43	39	24	6	12	106	67	54	1.58
3 Tottenham Hotspur	42	10	6	5	43	24	11	5	5	43	26	21	11	10	86	50	53	1.72
4 West Bromwich Albion	42	12	4	5	48	25	7	7	7	35	32	19	11	12	83	57	49	1.46
5 Sheffield Wednesday	42	12	7	2	48	20	7	4	10	32	39	19	11	12	80	59	49	1.36
6 Bolton Wanderers	42	12	5	4	37	27	8	3	10	22	24	20	8	14	59	51	48	1.16
7 Manchester United	42	13	3	5	53	30	6	4	11	49	50	19	7	16	102	80	45	1.28
8 Newcastle United	42	10	5	6	42	32	8	3	10	40	46	18	8	16	82	78	44	1.05
9 Preston North End	42	10	6	5	43	34	6	6	9	36	42	16	12	14	79	76	44	1.04
10 Fulham	42	12	4	5	42	28	5	6	10	31	52	17	10	15	73	80	44	0.91
11 Blackpool	42	9	6	6	32	32	6	4	11	27	39	15	10	17	59	71	40	0.83
12 Leicester City	42	8	6	7	38	32	5	7	9	28	43	13	13	16	66	75	39	0.88
13 Arsenal	42	9	5	7	39	38	6	4	11	29	42	15	9	18	68	80	39	0.85
14 West Ham United	42	12	3	6	47	33	4	3	14	28	58	16	6	20	75	91	38	0.82
15 Everton	42	13	3	5	50	20	0	8	13	23	58	13	11	18	73	78	37	0.94
16 Manchester City	42	11	2	8	47	34	6	1	14	31	50	17	3	22	78	84	37	0.93
17 Blackburn Rovers	42	12	3	6	38	29	4	2	15	22	41	16	5	21	60	70	37	0.86
18 Chelsea	42	7	5	9	44	50	7	4	10	32	41	14	9	19	76	91	37	0.84
19 Birmingham City	42	9	5	7	37	36	4	5	12	26	44	13	10	19	63	80	36	0.79
20 Nottingham Forest	42	8	6	7	30	28	5	3	13	20	46	13	9	20	50	74	35	0.68
21 Leeds United	42	7	5	9	37	46	5	5	11	28	46	12	10	20	65	92	34	0.71
22 Luton Town	42	6	5	10	25	29	3	7	11	25	44	9	12	21	50	73	30	0.68

Season 1960/61

Date	Opponents	Result	Crowd	Scorers
20/08/1960	Liverpool (A)	0 - 2	43041	-
24/08/1960	Bristol Rovers (H)	1 - 1	11330	McCole
27/08/1960	Rotherham United (H)	2 - 0	16480	McCole, Hawksby
29/08/1960	Bristol Rovers (A)	4 - 4	18864	McCole, Peyton, Hawksby, Grainger
03/09/1960	Southampton (A)	4 - 2	21862	McCole, Cameron, Francis, Grainger
07/09/1960	Leyton Orient (H)	1 - 3	17363	Cameron
10/09/1960	Huddersfield Town (H)	1 - 4	22146	Cameron (pen)
14/09/1960	Leyton Orient (A)	1 - 0	8505	Revie
17/09/1960	Middlesbrough (H)	4 - 4	17799	OG, McCole, Goodwin, Cameron (pen)
24/09/1960	Brighton and Hove Albion (A)	1 - 2	16276	McCole
28/09/1960	Blackpool (LCR2) (H)	0 - 0	13064	-
01/10/1960	Ipswich Town (H)	2 - 5	13502	McCole (2)
05/10/1960	Blackpool (LCR2R) (A)	3 - 0 (aet)	9614	Revie, McCole, Grainger
08/10/1960	Sunderland (A)	3 - 2	22296	McCole, Peyton, Francis
15/10/1960	Plymouth Argyle (H)	2 - 1	12229	Francis, Grainger
22/10/1960	Norwich City (A)	2 - 3	18970	Bremner (2)
29/10/1960	Charlton Athletic (H)	1 - 0	14014	Grainger
05/11/1960	Sheffield United (A)	2 - 3	17565	Francis, Cameron (pen)
12/11/1960	Stoke City (H)	0 - 1	13486	-
19/11/1960	Swansea City (A)	2 - 3	11140	McCole, Cameron
23/11/1960	Chesterfield (LCR3) (A)	4 - 0	2021	McCole, Peyton, Bremner, Cameron (pen)
03/12/1960	Lincoln City (A)	3 - 2	5678	McCole, Peyton, Bremner
05/12/1960	Southampton (LCR4) (A)	4 - 5	13448	McCole, Peyton, Charlton, Cameron (pen)
10/12/1960	Portsmouth (H)	0 - 0	9421	-
17/12/1960	Liverpool (H)	2 - 2	11929	Murray, Bremner
24/12/1960	Derby County (A)	3 - 2	15185	McCole, Bremner (2)
27/12/1960	Derby County (H)	3 - 3	18517	McCole, Murray, Charlton
31/12/1960	Rotherham United (A)	3 - 1	12557	OG (2) McCole
07/01/1961	Sheffield Wednesday (FACR3) (A)	0 - 2	34821	-
14/01/1961	Southampton (H)	3 - 0	14039	Cameron, Francis (2)
21/01/1961	Huddersfield Town (A)	1 - 0	18938	McCole

04/02/1961	Middlesbrough (A)	0 - 3	16593	-
10/02/1961	Brighton and Hove Albion (H)	3 - 2	12598	McCole, Goodwin, Charlton
18/02/1961	Ipswich Town (A)	0 - 4	13125	-
25/02/1961	Sunderland (H)	2 - 4	15136	Smith, Bremner
04/03/1961	Plymouth Argyle (A)	1 - 3	14878	Grainger
08/03/1961	Luton Town (H)	1 - 2	9995	Cameron (pen)
11/03/1961	Norwich City (H)	1 - 0	11294	Smith
18/03/1961	Portsmouth (A)	1 - 3	16230	Charlton
25/03/1961	Sheffield United (H)	1 - 2	13688	OG
01/04/1961	Luton Town (A)	1 - 1	11137	Bremner
03/04/1961	Scunthorpe United (A)	2 - 3	8725	Charlton (2, 1 pen)
08/04/1961	Swansea City (H)	2 - 2	11862	Charlton (2)
15/04/1961	Stoke City (A)	0 - 0	7130	-
22/04/1961	Lincoln City (H)	7 - 0	8432	OG, Bell, McCole (2, 1pen), Peyton, Bremner, McConnell
25/04/1961	Scunthorpe United (H)	2 - 2	6975	McCole (2)
29/04/1961	Charlton Athletic (A)	0 - 2	9081	-

Division 2 Final Standings 1960/61	Pld	Home					Away					Overall					Pts	GA
		W	D	L	F	A	W	D	L	F	A	W	D	L	F	A		
1 Ipswich Town	42	15	3	3	55	24	11	4	6	45	31	26	7	9	100	55	59	1.82
2 Sheffield United	42	16	2	3	49	22	10	4	7	32	29	26	6	10	81	51	58	1.59
3 Liverpool	42	14	5	2	49	21	7	5	9	38	37	21	10	11	87	58	52	1.50
4 Norwich City	42	15	3	3	46	20	5	6	10	24	33	20	9	13	70	53	49	1.32
5 Middlesbrough	42	13	6	2	44	20	5	6	10	39	54	18	12	12	83	74	48	1.12
6 Sunderland	42	12	5	4	47	24	5	8	8	28	36	17	13	12	75	60	47	1.25
7 Swansea Town	42	14	4	3	49	26	4	7	10	28	47	18	11	13	77	73	47	1.05
8 Southampton	42	12	4	5	57	35	6	4	11	27	46	18	8	16	84	81	44	1.04
9 Scunthorpe United	42	9	8	4	39	25	5	7	9	30	39	14	15	13	69	64	43	1.08
10 Charlton Athletic	42	12	3	6	60	42	4	8	9	37	49	16	11	15	97	91	43	1.07
11 Plymouth Argyle	42	13	4	4	52	32	4	4	13	29	50	17	8	17	81	82	42	0.99
12 Derby County	42	9	6	6	46	35	6	4	11	34	45	15	10	17	80	80	40	1.00
13 Luton Town	42	13	5	3	48	27	2	4	15	23	52	15	9	18	71	79	39	0.90
14 Leeds United	**42**	**7**	**7**	**7**	**41**	**38**	**7**	**3**	**11**	**34**	**45**	**14**	**10**	**18**	**75**	**83**	**38**	**0.90**
15 Rotherham United	42	9	7	5	37	24	3	6	12	28	40	12	13	17	65	64	37	1.02
16 Brighton & Hove Albion	42	9	6	6	33	26	5	3	13	28	49	14	9	19	61	75	37	0.81
17 Bristol Rovers	42	13	4	4	52	35	2	3	16	21	57	15	7	20	73	92	37	0.79
18 Stoke City	42	9	6	6	39	26	3	6	12	12	33	12	12	18	51	59	36	0.86
19 Leyton Orient	42	10	5	6	31	29	4	3	14	24	49	14	8	20	55	78	36	0.71
20 Huddersfield Town	42	7	5	9	33	33	6	4	11	29	38	13	9	20	62	71	35	0.87
21 Portsmouth	42	10	6	5	38	27	1	5	15	26	64	11	11	20	64	91	33	0.70
22 Lincoln City	42	5	4	12	30	43	3	4	14	18	52	8	8	26	48	95	24	0.51

Season 1961/62

Date	Opponents	Result	Crowd	Scorers
19/08/1961	Charlton Athletic (H)	1 - 0	12916	Bremner
22/08/1961	Brighton and Hove Albion (A)	3 - 1	22744	Mayers, Peyton, Bremner
26/08/1961	Liverpool (A)	0 - 5	42450	-
30/08/1961	Brighton and Hove Albion (H)	1 - 1	12642	Bremner
02/09/1961	Rotherham United (H)	1 - 3	12610	McCole
06/09/1961	Norwich City (A)	0 - 2	26860	-
09/09/1961	Sunderland (A)	1 - 2	30737	McCole
13/09/1961	Brentford (LCR1) (H)	4 - 1	4517	McCole (4)
16/09/1961	Stoke City (H)	3 - 1	9578	McCole, Peyton, Bremner
20/09/1961	Norwich City (H)	0 - 1	10948	-
23/09/1961	Bristol Rovers (A)	0 - 4	13676	-
30/09/1961	Preston North End (H)	1 - 2	9360	Charlton
04/10/1961	Huddersfield Town (LCR2) (H)	3 - 2	10023	Charlton, McConnell, Bremner (pen)
07/10/1961	Plymouth Argyle (A)	1 - 1	10144	McConnell
14/10/1961	Huddersfield Town (H)	1 - 0	19162	Charlton
21/10/1961	Swansea City (A)	1 - 2	11091	McConnell
28/10/1961	Southampton (H)	1 - 1	10145	McConnell
04/11/1961	Luton Town (A)	2 - 3	10341	Revie, Bremner (pen)
11/11/1961	Leyton Orient (H)	0 - 0	7967	-
18/11/1961	Middlesbrough (A)	3 - 1	10758	Mayers, Bremner, Charlton
25/11/1961	Walsall (H)	4 - 1	10999	Peyton, Charlton (2), Bremner (pen)
02/12/1961	Derby County (A)	3 - 3	16408	Bell, Mayers, Peyton
12/12/1961	Rotherham United (LCR4) (A)	1 - 1	10899	Charlton
16/12/1961	Charlton Athletic (A)	1 - 3	9459	Bremner (pen)
23/12/1961	Liverpool (H)	1 - 0	17214	Bremner
26/12/1961	Scunthorpe United (H)	1 - 4	19481	Charlton
06/01/1962	Derby County (FACR3) (H)	2 - 2	27089	Peyton, Charlton
10/01/1962	Derby County (FACR3R) (A)	1 - 3	28168	McAdams
12/01/1962	Rotherham United (A)	1 - 2	6207	McAdams
15/01/1962	Rotherham United (LCR4R) (H)	1 - 2	6385	Johanneson (pen)
20/01/1962	Sunderland (H)	1 - 0	17763	Smith
27/01/1962	Newcastle United (H)	0 - 1	17120	-
03/02/1962	Stoke City (A)	1 - 2	21935	Peyton
10/02/1962	Bristol Rovers (H)	0 - 0	9108	-
20/02/1962	Scunthorpe United (A)	1 - 2	9186	Mayers (pen)

144

24/02/1962	Plymouth Argyle (H)	2 - 3	8554	Mayers, Charlton
03/03/1962	Huddersfield Town (A)	1 - 2	16799	Charlton
10/03/1962	Swansea City (H)	2 - 0	17314	Collins, McAdams
17/03/1962	Southampton (A)	1 - 4	11924	Lawson
24/03/1962	Luton Town (H)	2 - 1	13078	Bremner (2)
31/03/1962	Leyton Orient (A)	0 - 0	13290	-
07/04/1962	Middlesbrough (H)	2 - 0	16116	OG, Hair
09/04/1962	Preston North End (A)	1 - 1	10492	OG
14/04/1962	Walsall (A)	1 - 1	9005	Johanneson
20/04/1962	Bury (A)	1 - 1	11313	Charlton
21/04/1962	Derby County (H)	0 - 0	11922	-
24/04/1962	Bury (H)	0 - 0	21482	-
28/04/1962	Newcastle United (A)	3 - 0	21708	OG, McAdams, Johanneson

Division 2 Final Standings 1961/62	Pld	Home					Away					Overall					Pts	GA
		W	D	L	F	A	W	D	L	F	A	W	D	L	F	A		
1 Liverpool	42	18	3	0	68	19	9	5	7	31	24	27	8	7	99	43	62	2.30
2 Leyton Orient	42	11	5	5	34	17	11	5	5	35	23	22	10	10	69	40	54	1.73
3 Sunderland	42	17	3	1	60	16	5	6	10	25	34	22	9	11	85	50	53	1.70
4 Scunthorpe United	42	14	4	3	52	26	7	3	11	34	45	21	7	14	86	71	49	1.21
5 Plymouth Argyle	42	12	4	5	45	30	7	4	10	30	45	19	8	15	75	75	46	1.00
6 Southampton	42	13	3	5	53	28	5	6	10	24	34	18	9	15	77	62	45	1.24
7 Huddersfield Town	42	11	5	5	39	22	5	7	9	28	37	16	12	14	67	59	44	1.14
8 Stoke City	42	13	4	4	34	17	4	4	13	21	40	17	8	17	55	57	42	0.96
9 Rotherham United	42	9	6	6	36	30	7	3	11	34	46	16	9	17	70	76	41	0.92
10 Preston North End	42	11	4	6	34	23	4	6	11	21	34	15	10	17	55	57	40	0.96
11 Newcastle United	42	10	5	6	40	27	5	4	12	24	31	15	9	18	64	58	39	1.10
12 Middlesbrough	42	11	3	7	45	29	5	4	12	31	43	16	7	19	76	72	39	1.06
13 Luton Town	42	12	1	8	44	37	5	4	12	25	34	17	5	20	69	71	39	0.97
14 Walsall	42	11	7	3	42	23	3	4	14	28	52	14	11	17	70	75	39	0.93
15 Charlton Athletic	42	10	5	6	38	30	5	4	12	31	45	15	9	18	69	75	39	0.92
16 Derby County	42	10	7	4	42	27	4	4	13	26	48	14	11	17	68	75	39	0.91
17 Norwich City	42	10	6	5	36	28	4	5	12	25	42	14	11	17	61	70	39	0.87
18 Bury	42	9	4	8	32	36	8	1	12	20	40	17	5	20	52	76	39	0.68
19 Leeds United	**42**	**9**	**6**	**6**	**24**	**19**	**3**	**6**	**12**	**26**	**42**	**12**	**12**	**18**	**50**	**61**	**36**	**0.82**
20 Swansea Town	42	10	5	6	38	30	2	7	12	23	53	12	12	18	61	83	36	0.73
21 Bristol Rovers	42	11	3	7	36	31	2	4	15	17	50	13	7	22	53	81	33	0.65
22 Brighton & Hove Albion	42	7	7	7	24	32	3	4	14	18	54	10	11	21	42	86	31	0.49

Carlisle United in the McConnell Years:

Season 1962/63

Date	Opponents	Result	Crowd	Scorers
Tue 21 Aug	Peterborough United (H)	1-4	12,238	Stark
Fri 24 Aug	Queens Park Rangers (H)	2-5	8,116	Stark, Taylor
Mon 27 Aug	Peterborough United (A)	2-2	13,668	Stark, Walker
Fri 31 Aug	Hull City (A)	1-3	8,325	Stark
Mon 03 Sep	Tranmere Rovers (A) LgCR1	3-2	5,446	Grant (3)
Sat 08 Sep	Crystal Palace (H)	2-2	6,591	Grant, Dagger
Wed 12 Sep	Bradford Park Avenue (A)	1-3	7,429	Dagger
Sat 15 Sep	Wrexham (A)	1-2	9,378	Dagger
Tue 18 Sep	Swindon Town (H)	0-0	6,602	-
Sat 22 Sep	Halifax Town (H)	1-0	4,895	Walker
Wed 26 Sep	Torquay United (A) LgCR2	2-1	3,899	Walker, Taylor
Sat 29 Sep	Bristol Rovers (A)	1-1	9,104	Stark
Tue 02 Oct	Brighton & Hove Albion (H)	1-0	7,865	Dagger
Fri 05 Oct	Bristol City (H)	2-5	8,229	Dagger, Davies
Tue 09 Oct	Brighton & Hove Albion (A)	0-1	6,556	-
Fri 12 Oct	Reading (A)	0-2	12,922	-
Tue 16 Oct	Norwich City (H) LgCR3	1-1	8,105	Brayton
Sat 20 Oct	Port Vale (H)	1-1	5,627	Stark
Wed 24 Oct	Norwich City (A) LgCR3R	0-5	14,210	-
Sat 27 Oct	Shrewsbury Town (A)	1-1	5,368	Stark
Sat 03 Nov	Hartlepools United (H) FA1	2-1	6,627	Brayton, OG
Sat 10 Nov	Southend United (A)	0-2	8,856	-
Sat 17 Nov	Colchester United (H)	3-1	3,518	Brayton, Taylor, Thompson
Sat 24 Nov	Blyth Spartans (A) FA2	2-0	5,928	Walker, Brayton

Fri 30 Nov	Bournemouth & Boscombe Ath. (H)	0-3	6,903	-
Sat 08 Dec	Coventry City (A)	2-3	8,853	Blue, Taylor
Sat 15 Dec	Northampton Town (H)	1-2	3,933	McConnell (pen)
Sat 22 Dec	Queens Park Rangers (A)	2-2	9,733	Livingstone (2)
Wed 26 Dec	Watford (H)	2-1	5,479	Brayton, Livingstone
Sat 29 Dec	Watford (A)	1-5	8,397	McConnell (pen)
Tue 29 Jan	Gravesend & Northfleet (H) FA3	0-1	9,115	-
Sat 23 Feb	Bristol City (A)	2-2	8,413	Brayton (2)
Sat 09 Mar	Port Vale (A)	0-2	6,308	-
Tue 12 Mar	Notts. County (H)	4-2	6,732	Brayton, Kirkup, Livingstone, McIlmoyle
Sat 16 Mar	Shrewsbury Town (H)	2-1	4,825	Livingstone, McConnell
Thu 21 Mar	Notts. County (A)	0-1	3,455	-
Sat 23 Mar	Millwall (A)	0-2	10,005	-
Tue 26 Mar	Halifax Town (A)	4-2	2,735	Kirkup, Livingstone, McIlmoyle (2)
Sat 30 Mar	Southend United (H)	1-2	5,435	Livingstone
Tue 02 Apr	Bristol Rovers (H)	4-0	5,354	Livingstone, McIlmoyle, Brayton, Dagger
Sat 06 Apr	Colchester United (A)	1-2	4,282	Livingstone
Fri 12 Apr	Barnsley (H)	2-1	5,944	Davies, Livingstone
Tue 16 Apr	Barnsley (A)	0-2	8,146	-
Sat 20 Apr	Bournemouth & Boscombe Ath. (A)	1-5	8,899	Dagger
Tue 23 Apr	Bradford Park Avenue (H)	3-0	4,845	Brayton, Davies, Oliphant (pen)
Sat 27 Apr	Coventry City (H)	0-1	4,751	-
Tue 30 Apr	Swindon Town (A)	0-2	14,221	-
Mon 06 May	Reading (H)	1-1	4,305	Kirkup
Thu 09 May	Northampton Town (A)	0-2	15,062	-
Sat 11 May	Hull City (H)	2-1	2,519	Livingstone, McIlmoyle
Tue 14 May	Millwall (H)	4-3	3,292	Brayton, Livingstone, McIlmoyle, Oliphant

Sat 18 May	Crystal Palace (A)	0-3	10,242	-
Thu 23 May	Wrexham (H)	2-1	3,092	McIlmoyle (2)

Division 3 Final Standings 1962/63	Pld	Home					Away					Overall					Pts	GA
		W	D	L	F	A	W	D	L	F	A	W	D	L	F	A		
1 Northampton Town	46	16	6	1	64	19	10	4	9	45	41	26	10	10	109	60	62	1.82
2 Swindon Town	46	18	2	3	60	22	4	12	7	27	34	22	14	10	87	56	58	1.55
3 Port Vale	46	16	4	3	47	25	7	4	12	25	33	23	8	15	72	58	54	1.24
4 Coventry City	46	14	6	3	54	28	4	11	8	29	41	18	17	11	83	69	53	1.20
5 Bournemouth & Bosc. Ath.	46	11	12	0	39	16	7	4	12	24	30	18	16	12	63	46	52	1.37
6 Peterborough United	46	11	5	7	48	33	9	6	8	45	42	20	11	15	93	75	51	1.24
7 Notts. County	46	15	3	5	46	29	4	10	9	27	45	19	13	14	73	74	51	0.99
8 Southend United	46	11	7	5	38	24	8	5	10	37	53	19	12	15	75	77	50	0.97
9 Wrexham	46	14	6	3	54	27	6	3	14	30	56	20	9	17	84	83	49	1.01
10 Hull City	46	12	6	5	40	22	7	4	12	34	47	19	10	17	74	69	48	1.07
11 Crystal Palace	46	10	7	6	38	22	7	6	10	30	36	17	13	16	68	58	47	1.17
12 Colchester United	46	11	6	6	41	35	7	5	11	32	58	18	11	17	73	93	47	0.78
13 Queens Park Rangers	46	9	6	8	44	36	8	5	10	41	40	17	11	18	85	76	45	1.12
14 Bristol City	46	10	9	4	54	38	6	4	13	46	54	16	13	17	100	92	45	1.09
15 Shrewsbury Town	46	13	4	6	57	41	3	8	12	26	40	16	12	18	83	81	44	1.02
16 Millwall	46	11	6	6	50	32	4	7	12	32	55	15	13	18	82	87	43	0.94
17 Watford	46	12	3	8	55	40	5	5	13	27	45	17	8	21	82	85	42	0.96
18 Barnsley	46	12	6	5	39	28	3	5	15	24	46	15	11	20	63	74	41	0.85
19 Bristol Rovers	46	11	8	4	45	29	4	3	16	25	59	15	11	20	70	88	41	0.80
20 Reading	46	13	4	6	51	30	3	4	16	23	48	16	8	22	74	78	40	0.95
21 Bradford Park Avenue	46	10	9	4	43	36	4	3	16	36	61	14	12	20	79	97	40	0.81
22 Brighton & Hove Albion	46	7	6	10	28	38	5	6	12	30	46	12	12	22	58	84	36	0.69
23 Carlisle United	46	12	4	7	41	37	1	5	17	20	52	13	9	24	61	89	35	0.69
24 Halifax Town	46	8	3	12	41	51	1	9	13	23	55	9	12	25	64	106	30	0.60

Season 1963/64

Date	Opponents	Result	Crowd	Scorers
Sat 24 Aug	Darlington (H)	3-3	5,782	McIlmoyle (2), Livingstone
Mon 26 Aug	Exeter City (H)	3-0	6,454	McIlmoyle (2), Livingstone
Fri 30 Aug	Tranmere Rovers (A)	1-6	9,086	McIlmoyle
Wed 04 Sep	Crewe Alexandra (H) LgCR1	3-2	5,874	Johnstone, Livingstone, McIlmoyle
Sat 07 Sep	Halifax Town (H)	3-0	5,224	Livingstone (2), Davies
Wed 11 Sep	Exeter City (A)	0-1	5,671	-
Sat 14 Sep	Torquay United (A)	1-3	4,680	McIlmoyle
Mon 16 Sep	Hartlepools United (A)	6-0	3,815	McIlmoyle (2), Johnstone, Davies, Brayton, OG
Fri 20 Sep	Oxford United (H)	2-1	7,196	McIlmoyle, OG
Wed 25 Sep	Manchester City (A) LgCR2	0-2	37,916	-
Fri 27 Sep	Aldershot (H)	4-0	3,144	Kirkup (3), McIlmoyle
Tue 01 Oct	Hartlepools United (H)	7-1	7,075	McIlmoyle (4), Brayton (2), McConnell
Sat 05 Oct	Bradford City (A)	2-2	3,658	McIlmoyle, Brayton
Wed 09 Oct	Gillingham (A)	0-2	17,421	
Sat 12 Oct	Newport County (A)	4-1	5,489	McConnell (2), McIlmoyle, Kirkup
Tue 15 Oct	Gillingham (H)	3-1	11,900	McIlmoyle (3)
Fri 18 Oct	Stockport County (H)	0-0	9,507	-
Tue 22 Oct	Lincoln City (H)	5-0	10,257	Livingstone (3), Davies, OG
Sat 26 Oct	Bradford Park Avenue (A)	1-1	6,448	Livingstone
Wed 30 Oct	Lincoln City (A)	2-0	7,013	McIlmoyle (2)
Sat 02 Nov	Chesterfield (H)	1-0	8,223	Kirkup
Sat 09 Nov	Doncaster Rovers (A)	1-1	5,397	Davies (pen)

149

Sat 16 Nov	York City (A) FA1	5-2	7,343	Livingstone, McIlmoyle, Davies (pen), Kirkup, Taylor
Sat 23 Nov	Chester (A)	2-4	8,223	Livingstone, McIlmoyle
Sat 30 Nov	York City (H)	4-0	5,884	McIlmoyle (2), Brayton, Davies
Sat 07 Dec	Gateshead (H) FA2	4-3	12,719	McIlmoyle (3), Taylor
Sat 14 Dec	Darlington (A)	6-1	3,075	Livingstone (3), McIlmoyle (2), McConnell
Sat 21 Dec	Tranmere Rovers (H)	5-2	6,671	McIlmoyle (3), Livingstone, Brayton
Thu 26 Dec	Workington (A)	2-2	18,633	Livingstone (2)
Sat 28 Dec	Workington (H)	3-1	16,347	McIlmoyle, Taylor, Davies
Sat 04 Jan	Queens Park Rangers (H) FA3	2-0	15,359	Livingstone, McIlmoyle
Sat 11 Jan	Halifax Town (A)	2-1	3,389	Livingstone, Kirkup
Sat 18 Jan	Torquay United (H)	0-1	9,844	-
Sat 25 Jan	Bedford Town (A) FA4	3-0	18,000	Livingstone, Kirkup, Davies (pen)
Sat 01 Feb	Oxford United (A)	2-1	10,546	McIlmoyle, Davies (pen)
Tue 04 Feb	Bradford City (H)	1-2	9,914	Evans
Sat 08 Feb	Aldershot (A)	2-3	5,135	McConnell, OG
Sat 15 Feb	Preston North End (A) FA5	0-1	37,100	-
Sat 22 Feb	Newport County (H)	3-3	7,528	McIlmoyle (2), Livingstone
Mon 24 Feb	Brighton & Hove Albion (H)	0-1	8,506	-
Sat 29 Feb	Stockport County (A)	3-0	3,645	Thompson, McIlmoyle, Evans
Sat 07 Mar	Bradford Park Avenue (H)	4-0	7,175	Evans (2), McIlmoyle, McConnell
Sat 21 Mar	Doncaster Rovers (H)	6-0	4,753	Evans (3), McIlmoyle, Davies, Taylor
Fri 27 Mar	Southport (H)	5-2	9,557	Evans (2), Davies (pen), McConnell, Livingstone
Sat 28 Mar	Rochdale (A)	1-1	2,736	Livingstone
Mon 30 Mar	Southport (A)	0-3	3,778	-

Sat 04 Apr	Chester (H)	3-1	6,940	McIlmoyle (2), Evans
Sat 11 Apr	York City (A)	0-0	3,151	-
Fri 17 Apr	Barrow (H)	4-1	9,538	Evans (2), Livingstone (2)
Tue 21 Apr	Rochdale (H)	1-0	11,556	Evans
Sat 25 Apr	Brighton & Hove Albion (A)	3-1	8,773	Evans (2), McIlmoyle

Division 4 Final Standings 1963/64	Pld	Home					Away					Overall					Pts	GA
		W	D	L	F	A	W	D	L	F	A	W	D	L	F	A		
1 Gillingham	46	16	7	0	37	10	7	7	9	22	20	23	14	9	59	30	60	1.97
2 **Carlisle United**	46	17	3	3	70	20	8	7	8	43	38	25	10	11	113	58	60	1.95
3 Workington	46	15	6	2	46	19	9	5	9	30	33	24	11	11	76	52	59	1.46
4 Exeter City	46	12	9	2	39	14	8	9	6	23	23	20	18	8	62	37	58	1.68
5 Bradford City	46	15	3	5	45	24	10	3	10	31	38	25	6	15	76	62	56	1.23
6 Torquay United	46	16	6	1	60	20	4	5	14	20	34	20	11	15	80	54	51	1.48
7 Tranmere Rovers	46	12	4	7	46	30	8	7	8	39	43	20	11	15	85	73	51	1.16
8 Brighton & Hove Albion	46	13	3	7	45	22	6	9	8	26	30	19	12	15	71	52	50	1.37
9 Aldershot	46	15	3	5	58	28	4	7	12	25	50	19	10	17	83	78	48	1.06
10 Halifax Town	46	14	4	5	47	28	3	10	10	30	49	17	14	15	77	77	48	1.00
11 Lincoln City	46	15	2	6	49	31	4	7	12	18	44	19	9	18	67	75	47	0.89
12 Chester	46	17	3	3	47	18	2	5	16	18	42	19	8	19	65	60	46	1.08
13 Bradford Park Avenue	46	13	5	5	50	34	5	4	14	25	47	18	9	19	75	81	45	0.93
14 Doncaster Rovers	46	11	8	4	46	23	4	4	15	24	52	15	12	19	70	75	42	0.93
15 Newport County	46	12	3	8	35	24	5	5	13	29	49	17	8	21	64	73	42	0.88
16 Chesterfield	46	8	9	6	29	27	7	3	13	28	44	15	12	19	57	71	42	0.80
17 Stockport County	46	12	7	4	32	19	3	5	15	18	49	15	12	19	50	68	42	0.74
18 Oxford United	46	10	7	6	37	27	4	6	13	22	36	14	13	19	59	63	41	0.94
19 Darlington	46	8	9	6	40	37	6	3	14	26	56	14	12	20	66	93	40	0.71
20 Rochdale	46	9	8	6	36	24	3	7	13	20	35	12	15	19	56	59	39	0.95
21 Southport	46	12	6	5	42	29	3	3	17	21	59	15	9	22	63	88	39	0.72
22 York City	46	9	3	11	29	26	5	4	14	23	40	14	7	25	52	66	35	0.79
23 Hartlepools United	46	8	7	8	30	36	4	2	17	24	57	12	9	25	54	93	33	0.58
24 Barrow	46	4	10	9	30	36	2	8	13	21	57	6	18	22	51	93	30	0.55

Season 1964/65

Date	Opponents	Result	Crowd	Scorers
Sat 22 Aug	Colchester United (A)	1-0	4,420	McIlmoyle
Mon 24 Aug	Port Vale (H)	1-1	11,809	Oliphant
Fri 28 Aug	Brentford (H)	0-1	11,023	-
Mon 31 Aug	Port Vale (A)	3-1	8,003	Brayton, Johnstone, McConnell
Wed 02 Sep	Southport (A) LgCR1	0-0	6,321	-
Sat 05 Sep	Bristol Rovers (A)	2-5	12,580	Livingstone (2)
Tue 08 Sep	Watford (H)	1-1	8,817	OG
Sat 12 Sep	Oldham Athletic (H)	2-0	9,618	Brayton, Harland
Mon 14 Sep	Southport (H) LgCR1R	1-0	8,349	Livingstone
Thu 17 Sep	Watford (A)	0-0	9,387	-
Sat 19 Sep	Exeter City (A)	0-0	7,368	-
Wed 23 Sep	Bristol City (H) LgCR2	4-1	10,055	McIlmoyle (2), Murray, Johnstone
Sat 26 Sep	Bournemouth & Boscombe Ath. (H)	3-4	8,708	Brayton, Johnstone, McConnell
Thu 01 Oct	Luton Town (A)	1-1	7,745	Large
Sat 03 Oct	Peterborough United (A)	2-1	11,012	Brayton, Evans
Wed 07 Oct	Luton Town (H)	1-1	9,038	Evans
Fri 09 Oct	Hull City (A)	0-1	10,931	-
Wed 14 Oct	Chesterfield (A) LgCR3	1-3	7,321	McConnell
Sat 17 Oct	Gillingham (H)	3-1	7,342	Evans, Large, McConnell
Wed 21 Oct	Grimsby Town (A)	1-1	5,345	Evans
Fri 23 Oct	Bristol City (A)	2-1	10,303	Evans, Kirkup
Tue 27 Oct	Walsall (H)	2-1	10,188	Evans, Kirkup
Fri 30 Oct	Queens Park Rangers (H)	2-0	9,483	Blain, Kirkup
Sat 07 Nov	Shrewsbury Town (A)	2-2	5,416	Large, McConnell

Sat 14 Nov	Crook Town (A) FA1	0-1	4,600	-
Sat 21 Nov	Southend United (A)	0-1	6,422	-
Sat 28 Nov	Barnsley (H)	4-0	6,723	Carlin, Evans, Large, Neil
Sat 05 Dec	Walsall (A)	0-1	5,578	-
Sat 12 Dec	Colchester United (H)	4-1	5,747	Large (2), Blain, McConnell
Sat 19 Dec	Brentford (A)	1-6	8,400	Large
Sat 26 Dec	Workington (H)	1-0	14,142	Large
Mon 28 Dec	Workington (A)	1-0	11,900	McConnell
Sat 02 Jan	Bristol Rovers (H)	1-2	11,311	Evans
Sat 09 Jan	Grimsby Town (H)	3-1	7,144	Blain, McConnell, Simpson
Sat 16 Jan	Oldham Athletic (A)	3-2	4,950	Evans (2), Simpson
Fri 29 Jan	Scunthorpe United (A)	1-0	6,710	Carlin
Sat 06 Feb	Bournemouth & Boscombe Ath. (A)	4-0	6,841	Evans (2), Large, OG
Sat 13 Feb	Peterborough United (H)	2-1	9,845	Blain, Simpson
Sat 20 Feb	Hull City (H)	0-0	17,174	-
Sat 27 Feb	Gillingham (A)	0-1	14,384	-
Sat 06 Mar	Scunthorpe United (H)	3-1	9,481	Evans, Harland, Large
Tue 09 Mar	Exeter City (H)	2-1	11,544	Carlin, Large
Fri 12 Mar	Queens Park Rangers (A)	2-1	5,934	Blain, Evans
Tue 16 Mar	Reading (H)	1-2	11,864	Large
Fri 19 Mar	Shrewsbury Town (H)	2-1	10,435	Large, Livingstone
Sat 27 Mar	Reading (A)	2-1	6,356	Carlin, Evans
Fri 02 Apr	Southend United (H)	4-3	12,050	Evans (2), Large, Simpson
Sat 10 Apr	Barnsley (A)	2-1	2,919	Caldwell, Carlin
Fri 16 Apr	Bristol City (H)	1-1	16,069	Harland

Mon 19 Apr	Mansfield Town (A)	0-2	13,832	-
Tue 20 Apr	Mansfield Town (H)	3-0	18,764	Large (2), Evans

Division 3 Final Standings 1964/65	Pld	Home					Away					Overall					Pts	GA
		W	D	L	F	A	W	D	L	F	A	W	D	L	F	A		
1 Carlisle United	46	14	5	4	46	24	11	5	7	30	29	25	10	11	76	53	60	1.43
2 Bristol City	46	14	6	3	53	18	10	5	8	39	37	24	11	11	92	55	59	1.67
3 Mansfield Town	46	17	4	2	61	23	7	7	9	34	38	24	11	11	95	61	59	1.56
4 Hull City	46	14	6	3	51	25	9	6	8	40	32	23	12	11	91	57	58	1.60
5 Brentford	46	18	4	1	55	18	6	5	12	28	37	24	9	13	83	55	57	1.51
6 Bristol Rovers	46	14	7	2	52	21	6	8	9	30	37	20	15	11	82	58	55	1.41
7 Gillingham	46	16	5	2	45	13	7	4	12	25	37	23	9	14	70	50	55	1.40
8 Peterborough United	46	16	3	4	61	33	6	4	13	24	41	22	7	17	85	74	51	1.15
9 Watford	46	13	8	2	45	21	4	8	11	26	43	17	16	13	71	64	50	1.11
10 Grimsby Town	46	11	10	2	37	21	5	7	11	31	46	16	17	13	68	67	49	1.01
11 Bournemouth & Bosc. Ath.	46	12	4	7	40	24	6	7	10	32	39	18	11	17	72	63	47	1.14
12 Southend United	46	14	4	5	48	24	5	4	14	30	47	19	8	19	78	71	46	1.10
13 Reading	46	12	8	3	45	26	4	6	13	25	44	16	14	16	70	70	46	1.00
14 Queens Park Rangers	46	15	5	3	48	23	2	7	14	24	57	17	12	17	72	80	46	0.90
15 Workington	46	11	7	5	30	22	6	5	12	28	47	17	12	17	58	69	46	0.84
16 Shrewsbury Town	46	10	6	7	42	38	5	6	12	34	46	15	12	19	76	84	42	0.90
17 Exeter City	46	8	7	8	33	27	4	10	9	18	25	12	17	17	51	52	41	0.98
18 Scunthorpe United	46	9	8	6	42	27	5	4	14	23	45	14	12	20	65	72	40	0.90
19 Walsall	46	9	4	10	34	36	6	3	14	21	44	15	7	24	55	80	37	0.69
20 Oldham Athletic	46	10	3	10	40	39	3	7	13	21	44	13	10	23	61	83	36	0.73
21 Luton Town	46	6	8	9	32	36	5	3	15	19	58	11	11	24	51	94	33	0.54
22 Port Vale	46	7	6	10	27	33	2	8	13	14	43	9	14	23	41	76	32	0.54
23 Colchester United	46	7	6	10	30	34	3	4	16	20	55	10	10	26	50	89	30	0.56
24 Barnsley	46	8	5	10	33	31	1	6	16	21	59	9	11	26	54	90	29	0.60

Season 1965/66

Date	Opponents	Result	Crowd	Scorers
Sat 21 Aug	Norwich City (H)	4-1	11,954	Simpson (2, 1 pen), Balderstone, Large
Wed 25 Aug	Southampton (A)	0-1	21,928	-
Sat 28 Aug	Wolverhampton Wanderers (A)	0-3	18,943	-
Tue 31 Aug	Southampton (H)	1-0	15,260	Harland
Fri 03 Sep	Rotherham United (H)	1-0	12,551	Balderstone
Tue 07 Sep	Derby County (H)	2-1	16,566	Blain, Large
Sat 11 Sep	Manchester City (A)	1-2	22,891	Evans
Wed 15 Sep	Derby County (A)	1-3	11,047	Evans
Fri 17 Sep	Bristol City (H)	5-0	10,694	Livingstone (2), Balderstone, Harland. Blain
Tue 21 Sep	Charlton Athletic (A) LgCR1	1-4	11,627	Balderstone
Sat 25 Sep	Coventry City (A)	2-3	20,672	Balderstone (2)
Sat 02 Oct	Preston North End (H)	0-2	14,729	-
Sat 09 Oct	Charlton Athletic (A)	2-3	11,369	Balderstone, Livingstone
Sat 16 Oct	Plymouth Argyle (H)	1-3	10,471	Livingstone
Sat 23 Oct	Portsmouth (A)	1-4	14,406	Balderstone
Sat 30 Oct	Bolton Wanderers (H)	1-1	11,114	Evans
Sat 06 Nov	Ipswich Town (A)	0-1	10,772	-
Sat 13 Nov	Birmingham City (H)	1-0	10,243	Welsh
Sat 20 Nov	Leyton Orient (A)	1-2	3,678	Wilson
Sat 04 Dec	Huddersfield Town (A)	0-2	15,517	-
Sat 11 Dec	Crystal Palace (H)	3-1	9,577	Livingstone, Wilson, Welsh
Mon 27 Dec	Bury (H)	4-1	12,019	Wilson (2), Livingstone, Balderstone
Sat 01 Jan	Charlton Athletic (H)	3-1	11,489	Balderstone, Harland, Welsh

Sat 08 Jan	Birmingham City (A)	1-2	14,989	Wilson
Sat 15 Jan	Portsmouth (H)	2-1	9,636	McConnell, Balderstone (pen)
Sat 22 Jan	Crystal Palace (H) FA3	3-0	13,640	McConnell, Welsh, Wilson
Sat 29 Jan	Norwich City (A)	0-2	16,231	-
Sat 05 Feb	Wolverhampton Wanderers (H)	2-1	13,838	Harland, Garbutt
Sat 12 Feb	Shrewsbury Town (A) FA4	0-0	13,967	-
Tue 15 Feb	Shrewsbury Town (H) FA4R *after extra time*	1-1	17,841	OG
Mon 21 Feb	Shrewsbury Town (neutral) FA4R2 *after extra time and game played at Deepdale, Preston North End*	3-4	18,678	Balderstone, Wilson, Carlin
Sat 26 Feb	Manchester City (H)	1-2	9,327	Wilson
Tue 08 Mar	Middlesbrough (H)	2-1	13,459	Wilson, Carlin
Sat 12 Mar	Bristol City (A)	0-2	14,721	-
Mon 14 Mar	Plymouth Argyle (A)	0-0	12,104	-
Fri 18 Mar	Coventry City (H)	2-2	13,167	Welsh, Carlin
Sat 02 Apr	Ipswich Town (H)	3-1	7,555	McConnell, Welsh, Brayton
Fri 08 Apr	Cardiff City (A)	1-1	8,003	Carlin
Tue 12 Apr	Cardiff City (H)	2-0	11,252	McConnell, Wilson
Fri 15 Apr	Leyton Orient (H)	1-0	9,811	McConnell
Sat 23 Apr	Middlesbrough (A)	2-0	15,564	Wilson (2)
Mon 25 Apr	Preston North End (A)	1-2	13,766	Balderstone
Sat 30 Apr	Huddersfield Town (H)	2-0	13,688	Balderstone, Carlin
Wed 04 May	Bolton Wanderers (A)	0-4	6,506	-
Sat 07 May	Crystal Palace (A)	0-2	9,413	-
Tue 10 May	Bury (A)	1-2	4,747	Carlin
Thu 12 May	Rotherham United (A)	3-3	4,798	Wilson (2), Brayton

Division 2 Final Standings 1965/66	Pld	Home					Away					Overall					Pts	GA
		W	D	L	F	A	W	D	L	F	A	W	D	L	F	A		
1 Manchester City	42	14	7	0	40	14	8	8	5	36	30	22	15	5	76	44	59	1.73
2 Southampton	42	13	4	4	51	25	9	6	6	34	31	22	10	10	85	56	54	1.52
3 Coventry City	42	14	5	2	54	31	6	8	7	19	22	20	13	9	73	53	53	1.38
4 Huddersfield Town	42	12	7	2	35	12	7	6	8	27	24	19	13	10	62	36	51	1.72
5 Bristol City	42	9	10	2	27	15	8	7	6	36	33	17	17	8	63	48	51	1.31
6 Wolverhampton Wanderers	42	15	4	2	52	18	5	6	10	35	43	20	10	12	87	61	50	1.43
7 Rotherham United	42	12	6	3	48	29	4	8	9	27	45	16	14	12	75	74	46	1.01
8 Derby County	42	13	2	6	48	31	3	9	9	23	37	16	11	15	71	68	43	1.04
9 Bolton Wanderers	42	12	2	7	43	25	4	7	10	19	34	16	9	17	62	59	41	1.05
10 Birmingham City	42	10	6	5	41	29	6	3	12	29	46	16	9	17	70	75	41	0.93
11 Crystal Palace	42	11	7	3	29	16	3	6	12	18	36	14	13	15	47	52	41	0.90
12 Portsmouth	42	13	4	4	47	26	3	4	14	27	52	16	8	18	74	78	40	0.95
13 Norwich City	42	8	7	6	33	27	4	8	9	19	25	12	15	15	52	52	39	1.00
14 Carlisle United	**42**	**16**	**2**	**3**	**43**	**19**	**1**	**3**	**17**	**17**	**44**	**17**	**5**	**20**	**60**	**63**	**39**	**0.95**
15 Ipswich Town	42	12	6	3	38	23	3	3	15	20	43	15	9	18	58	66	39	0.88
16 Charlton Athletic	42	10	6	5	39	29	2	8	11	22	41	12	14	16	61	70	38	0.87
17 Preston North End	42	7	10	4	37	23	4	5	12	25	47	11	15	16	62	70	37	0.89
18 Plymouth Argyle	42	7	8	6	37	26	5	5	11	17	37	12	13	17	54	63	37	0.86
19 Bury	42	12	5	4	45	25	2	2	17	17	51	14	7	21	62	76	35	0.82
20 Cardiff City	42	10	3	8	37	35	2	7	12	34	56	12	10	20	71	91	34	0.78
21 Middlesbrough	42	8	8	5	36	28	2	5	14	22	58	10	13	19	58	86	33	0.67
22 Leyton Orient	42	3	9	9	19	36	2	4	15	19	44	5	13	24	38	80	23	0.48

Season 1966/67

Date	Opponents	Result	Crowd	Scorers
Sat 20 Aug	Crystal Palace (A)	2-4	11,374	Welsh (2)
Tue 23 Aug	Derby County (H)	0-0	13,347	-
Sat 27 Aug	Huddersfield Town (H)	2-1	10,322	Carlin (2)
Wed 31 Aug	Derby County (A)	1-0	12,296	Welsh
Sat 03 Sep	Cardiff City (A)	2-4	7,014	McConnell, Welsh
Wed 07 Sep	Bolton Wanderers (A)	0-3	15,105	-
Sat 10 Sep	Wolverhampton Wanderers (H)	1-3	11,359	Wilson
Wed 14 Sep	Tranmere Rovers (H) LgCR2	1-1	6,076	Marsland
Sat 17 Sep	Ipswich Town (A)	2-1	14,317	Marsland, Carlin
Wed 21 Sep	Tranmere Rovers (A) LgCR2R	2-0	5,422	Balderstone, Welsh
Sat 24 Sep	Bristol City (H)	2-1	9,948	McVitie, Carlin
Tue 27 Sep	Norwich City (H)	1-0	10,329	Wilson
Sat 01 Oct	Bury (A)	2-0	5,552	Wilson (2)
Wed 05 Oct	Southampton (A) LgCR3	3-3	13,317	Balderstone, Hartle, Wilson
Sat 08 Oct	Coventry City (H)	2-1	10,885	Garbutt, Wilson
Wed 12 Oct	Southampton (H) LgCR3R	2-1	13,275	Balderstone (2)
Sat 15 Oct	Norwich City (A)	0-2	11,540	-
Sat 22 Oct	Birmingham City (H)	2-0	10,900	Carlin, Wilson
Wed 26 Oct	Blackburn Rovers (H) LgCR4	4-0	14,054	Balderstone, Carlin, Wilson (2)
Sat 29 Oct	Portsmouth (A)	1-2	11,674	Balderstone
Sat 05 Nov	Hull City (H)	2-0	14,157	Carlin, Wilson
Sat 12 Nov	Plymouth Argyle (A)	2-1	13,354	Carlin (2)
Sat 19 Nov	Northampton Town (H)	2-0	11,946	McVitie, Garbutt
Sat 26 Nov	Millwall (A)	1-2	15,895	Welsh

Sat 03 Dec	Rotherham United (H)	2-3	10,766	Garbutt, Welsh
Wed 07 Dec	Queens Park Rangers (A) LgCR5	1-2	19,146	Carlin
Sat 10 Dec	Preston North End (A)	3-2	15,869	Balderstone (2), Carlin
Sat 17 Dec	Crystal Palace (H)	3-0	10,324	Neil, Carlin, Wilson
Mon 26 Dec	Blackburn Rovers (H)	1-2	17,523	Welsh
Tue 27 Dec	Blackburn Rovers (A)	0-2	20,219	-
Sat 31 Dec	Huddersfield Town (A)	1-1	18,606	Rudge
Sat 07 Jan	Cardiff City (H)	3-0	10,295	Welsh (2), Wilson
Sat 14 Jan	Wolverhampton Wanderers (A)	1-1	23,522	McVitie
Sat 21 Jan	Ipswich Town (H)	2-1	11,812	Balderstone, Hartle
Sat 28 Jan	Blackburn Rovers (A) FA3	2-1	23,312	Wilson, Carlin
Sat 04 Feb	Bristol City (A)	0-3	23,206	-
Sat 11 Feb	Bury (H)	2-0	11,534	McConnell, McVitie
Sat 18 Feb	Ipswich Town (A) FA4	0-2	22,911	-
Sat 25 Feb	Coventry City (A)	1-2	29,965	McVitie
Sat 04 Mar	Portsmouth (H)	5-1	11,104	McConnell, Balderstone, Welsh, Rudge, McVitie
Sat 18 Mar	Birmingham City (A)	2-1	17,613	Welsh, McVitie
Fri 24 Mar	Charlton Athletic (A)	0-1	15,075	-
Tue 28 Mar	Charlton Athletic (H)	1-0	11,607	Murray
Sat 01 Apr	Hull City (A)	2-1	19,029	Garbutt, Welsh
Sat 08 Apr	Plymouth Argyle (H)	0-0	11,391	-
Sat 15 Apr	Northampton Town (A)	3-3	10,752	Murray, Rudge, Balderstone
Sat 22 Apr	Millwall (H)	2-1	8,493	Balderstone (pen), McVitie
Sat 29 Apr	Rotherham United (A)	3-2	7,641	McConnell, Murray, Rudge
Sat 06 May	Preston North End (H)	1-1	9,443	Welsh
Sat 13 May	Bolton Wanderers (H)	6-1	7,732	Rudge (3), Murray, Welsh, Gallacher

Division 2 Final Standings 1966/67	Pld	Home					Away					Overall					Pts	GA
		W	D	L	F	A	W	D	L	F	A	W	D	L	F	A		
1 Coventry City	42	17	3	1	46	16	6	10	5	28	27	23	13	6	74	43	59	1.72
2 Wolverhampton Wanderers	42	15	4	2	53	20	10	4	7	35	28	25	8	9	88	48	58	1.83
3 Carlisle United	**42**	**15**	**3**	**3**	**42**	**16**	**8**	**3**	**10**	**29**	**38**	**23**	**6**	**13**	**71**	**54**	**52**	**1.31**
4 Blackburn Rovers	42	13	6	2	33	11	6	7	8	23	35	19	13	10	56	46	51	1.22
5 Ipswich Town	42	11	8	2	45	25	6	8	7	25	29	17	16	9	70	54	50	1.30
6 Huddersfield Town	42	14	3	4	36	17	6	6	9	22	29	20	9	13	58	46	49	1.26
7 Crystal Palace	42	14	4	3	42	23	5	6	10	19	32	19	10	13	61	55	48	1.11
8 Millwall	42	14	5	2	33	17	4	4	13	16	41	18	9	15	49	58	45	0.84
9 Bolton Wanderers	42	10	7	4	36	19	4	7	10	28	39	14	14	14	64	58	42	1.10
10 Birmingham City	42	11	5	5	42	23	5	3	13	28	43	16	8	18	70	66	40	1.06
11 Norwich City	42	10	7	4	31	21	3	7	11	18	34	13	14	15	49	55	40	0.89
12 Hull City	42	11	5	5	46	25	5	2	14	31	47	16	7	19	77	72	39	1.07
13 Preston North End	42	14	3	4	44	23	2	4	15	21	44	16	7	19	65	67	39	0.97
14 Portsmouth	42	7	5	9	34	37	6	8	7	25	33	13	13	16	59	70	39	0.84
15 Bristol City	42	10	8	3	38	22	2	6	13	18	40	12	14	16	56	62	38	0.90
16 Plymouth Argyle	42	12	4	5	42	21	2	5	14	17	37	14	9	19	59	58	37	1.02
17 Derby County	42	8	6	7	40	32	4	6	11	28	40	12	12	18	68	72	36	0.94
18 Rotherham United	42	10	5	6	39	28	3	5	13	22	42	13	10	19	61	70	36	0.87
19 Charlton Athletic	42	11	4	6	34	16	2	5	14	15	37	13	9	20	49	53	35	0.92
20 Cardiff City	42	9	7	5	43	28	3	2	16	18	59	12	9	21	61	87	33	0.70
21 Northampton Town	42	8	6	7	28	33	4	0	17	19	51	12	6	24	47	84	30	0.56
22 Bury	42	9	3	9	31	30	2	3	16	18	53	11	6	25	49	83	28	0.59

Season 1967/68

Date	Opponents	Result	Crowd	Scorers
Sat 19 Aug	Hull City (A)	0-1	17,123	-
Wed 23 Aug	Blackburn Rovers (A)	0-1	17,740	-
Sat 26 Aug	Middlesbrough (H)	2-2	12,389	Garbutt, Balderstone
Tue 29 Aug	Blackburn Rovers (H)	1-0	11,668	Garbutt
Sat 02 Sep	Bristol City (A)	0-1	13,842	-
Tue 05 Sep	Rotherham United (H)	4-1	9,496	McCarron, Murray, Garbutt, OG
Sat 09 Sep	Birmingham City (H)	1-1	11,200	Garbutt
Wed 13 Sep	Workington (A) LgCR2	0-2	10,746	-

Sat 16 Sep	Bolton Wanderers (A)	3-2	12,809	McConnell (2), Murray
Sat 23 Sep	Huddersfield Town (H)	2-1	13,511	Marsland (pen), McIlmoyle
Sat 30 Sep	Ipswich Town (A)	1-3	14,183	Murray
Sat 07 Oct	Portsmouth (A)	1-2	21,865	McIlmoyle
Sat 14 Oct	Preston North End (H)	4-1	11,228	McIlmoyle, Balderstone, Marsland, Rudge
Sat 21 Oct	Charlton Athletic (A)	2-2	13,645	McIlmoyle, Balderstone
Sat 28 Oct	Crystal Palace (H)	3-0	11,399	Rudge (2), McIlmoyle
Sat 04 Nov	Aston Villa (A)	0-1	17,767	-
Sat 11 Nov	Queens Park Rangers (H)	3-1	12,544	Rudge, McIlmoyle (2)
Sat 18 Nov	Derby County (A)	1-0	20,850	Balderstone
Sat 25 Nov	Cardiff City (H)	1-3	10,966	McIlmoyle
Sat 02 Dec	Plymouth Argyle (A)	1-3	8,791	Rudge
Sat 09 Dec	Norwich City (H)	2-2	8,076	Murray (2)
Sat 16 Dec	Hull City (H)	1-1	9,063	Murray
Sat 23 Dec	Middlesbrough (A)	0-4	27,952	-
Tue 26 Dec	Blackpool (A)	1-1	20,732	McVitie
Sat 30 Dec	Blackpool (H)	1-3	12,679	Murray
Sat 06 Jan	Bristol City (H)	0-0	8,261	-
Sat 13 Jan	Birmingham City (A)	3-1	21,686	Rudge, Murray, McVitie
Sat 20 Jan	Bolton Wanderers (H)	3-0	11,065	Rudge, Murray, Barton
Sat 27 Jan	Newcastle United (A) FA3	1-0	56,550	Murray
Sat 03 Feb	Huddersfield Town (A)	1-1	9,071	OG
Sat 10 Feb	Ipswich Town (H)	4-1	17,111	Murray (2), Balderstone, Barton
Sat 17 Feb	Everton (H) FA4	0-2	25,000	-
Fri 23 Feb	Portsmouth (H)	1-1	11,976	Rudge

Sat 02 Mar	Preston North End (A)	2-0	13,481	Murray (2)
Sat 16 Mar	Charlton Athletic (H)	0-0	7,440	-
Sat 23 Mar	Crystal Palace (A)	1-1	9,219	Marsland
Sat 30 Mar	Aston Villa (H)	1-2	8,861	Garbutt
Sat 06 Apr	Queens Park Rangers (A)	0-1	18,103	-
Sat 13 Apr	Derby County (H)	1-1	8,009	McIlmoyle
Mon 15 Apr	Millwall (A)	0-1	11,854	-
Tue 16 Apr	Millwall (H)	1-1	5,810	McIlmoyle
Sat 20 Apr	Cardiff City (A)	0-1	13,926	-
Sat 27 Apr	Plymouth Argyle (H)	2-0	5,938	Murray, McVitie
Sat 04 May	Norwich City (A)	1-2	11,429	Rudge
Sat 11 May	Rotherham United (A)	2-1	6,950	McIlmoyle, Murray

Division 2 Final Standings 1967/68		Pld	Home					Away					Overall					Pts	GA
			W	D	L	F	A	W	D	L	F	A	W	D	L	F	A		
1	Ipswich Town	42	12	7	2	45	20	10	8	3	34	24	22	15	5	79	44	59	1.80
2	Queens Park Rangers	42	18	2	1	45	9	7	6	8	22	27	25	8	9	67	36	58	1.86
3	Blackpool	42	12	6	3	33	16	12	4	5	38	27	24	10	8	71	43	58	1.65
4	Birmingham City	42	12	6	3	54	21	7	8	6	29	30	19	14	9	83	51	52	1.63
5	Portsmouth	42	13	6	2	43	18	5	7	9	25	37	18	13	11	68	55	49	1.24
6	Middlesbrough	42	10	7	4	39	19	7	5	9	21	35	17	12	13	60	54	46	1.11
7	Millwall	42	9	10	2	35	16	5	7	9	27	34	14	17	11	62	50	45	1.24
8	Blackburn Rovers	42	13	5	3	34	16	3	6	12	22	33	16	11	15	56	49	43	1.14
9	Norwich City	42	12	4	5	40	30	4	7	10	20	35	16	11	15	60	65	43	0.92
10	**Carlisle United**	42	9	9	3	38	22	5	4	12	20	30	14	13	15	58	52	41	1.12
11	Crystal Palace	42	11	4	6	34	19	3	7	11	22	37	14	11	17	56	56	39	1.00
12	Bolton Wanderers	42	8	6	7	37	28	5	7	9	23	35	13	13	16	60	63	39	0.95
13	Cardiff City	42	9	6	6	35	29	4	6	11	25	37	13	12	17	60	66	38	0.91
14	Huddersfield Town	42	10	6	5	29	23	3	6	12	17	38	13	12	17	46	61	38	0.75
15	Charlton Athletic	42	10	6	5	43	25	2	7	12	20	43	12	13	17	63	68	37	0.93
16	Aston Villa	42	10	3	8	35	30	5	4	12	19	34	15	7	20	54	64	37	0.84
17	Hull City	42	6	8	7	25	23	6	5	10	33	50	12	13	17	58	73	37	0.79
18	Derby County	42	8	5	8	40	35	5	5	11	31	43	13	10	19	71	78	36	0.91
19	Bristol City	42	7	7	7	26	25	6	3	12	22	37	13	10	19	48	62	36	0.77
20	Preston North End	42	8	7	6	29	24	4	4	13	14	41	12	11	19	43	65	35	0.66
21	Rotherham United	42	7	4	10	22	32	3	7	11	20	44	10	11	21	42	76	31	0.55
22	Plymouth Argyle	42	5	4	12	26	36	4	5	12	12	36	9	9	24	38	72	27	0.53

Season 1968/69

Date	Opponents	Result	Crowd	Scorers
Sat 10 Aug	Bury (A)	2-3	8,952	McIlmoyle, Murray
Tue 13 Aug	Portsmouth (H)	0-0	9,748	-
Sat 17 Aug	Charlton Athletic (H)	1-1	8,621	McIlmoyle
Sat 24 Aug	Middlesbrough (A)	0-1	22,392	-
Tue 27 Aug	Oxford United (H)	0-2	9,396	-
Sat 31 Aug	Huddersfield Town (H)	0-0	7,935	-
Wed 04 Sep	Cardiff City (H) LgCR2	2-0	7,720	McIlmoyle, McVitie
Sat 07 Sep	Crystal Palace (A)	0-5	15,169	-

Sat 14 Sep	Norwich City (H)	0-4	7,353	-
Sat 21 Sep	Cardiff City (A)	1-2	10,809	Murray
Tue 24 Sep	Leicester City (H) LgCR3	0-3	10,985	-
Sat 28 Sep	Birmingham City (H)	2-3	7,623	Murray, McIlmoyle
Mon 30 Sep	Preston North End (A)	2-2	14,984	McVitie, McIlmoyle
Sat 05 Oct	Bolton Wanderers (H)	1-1	8,846	Garbutt
Wed 09 Oct	Oxford United (A)	1-0	10,256	Balderstone
Sat 12 Oct	Blackburn Rovers (A)	2-0	12,101	McIlmoyle (2)
Sat 19 Oct	Blackpool (H)	1-0	10,519	McVitie
Sat 26 Oct	Aston Villa (A)	0-0	14,971	-
Mon 04 Nov	Hull City (H)	1-0	9,374	Murray
Sat 09 Nov	Sheffield United (A)	1-0	13,158	McIlmoyle
Sat 16 Nov	Fulham (H)	2-0	9,644	Balderstone, McIlmoyle
Sat 23 Nov	Derby County (A)	3-3	23,395	McVitie, Garbutt, Murray
Sat 30 Nov	Bristol City (H)	3-0	9,263	Mcilmoyle (2), Garbutt
Sat 07 Dec	Millwall (A)	1-1	12,767	Balderstone
Sat 14 Dec	Blackburn Rovers (H)	4-1	9,160	Balderstone, McVitie, Murray (2)
Sat 21 Dec	Blackpool (A)	0-1	11,169	-
Thu 26 Dec	Bolton Wanderers (A)	1-0	13,922	McIlmoyle
Sat 28 Dec	Aston Villa (H)	0-1	12,554	-
Sat 04 Jan	Chelsea (A) FA3	0-2	37,322	-
Sat 11 Jan	Hull City (A)	2-1	12,389	McIlmoyle, Balderstone
Sat 18 Jan	Sheffield United (H)	0-1	9,717	-
Sat 01 Feb	Fulham (A)	2-0	12,863	Murray (2)
Sat 15 Feb	Bristol City (A)	0-3	13,785	-
Sat 22 Feb	Millwall (H)	1-0	7,937	McVitie

Sat 01 Mar	Bury (H)	2-0	7,937	McVitie, McIlmoyle
Sat 08 Mar	Charlton Athletic (A)	1-1	19,439	Barton
Tue 11 Mar	Derby County (H)	1-1	12,844	McIlmoyle
Sat 15 Mar	Middlesbrough (H)	3-0	13,920	Barton, Welsh, McIlmoyle
Sat 22 Mar	Huddersfield Town (A)	0-2	8,560	-
Sat 29 Mar	Crystal Palace (H)	1-2	8,172	Murray
Sat 05 Apr	Birmingham City (A)	0-3	22,397	-
Mon 07 Apr	Preston North End (H)	1-0	7,349	McIlmoyle
Wed 09 Apr	Portsmouth (A)	1-2	18,130	Murray
Sat 12 Apr	Cardiff City (H)	1-0	5,546	McIlmoyle
Sat 19 Apr	Norwich City (A)	1-2	8,313	Murray

Division 2 Final Standings 1968/69	Pld	Home					Away					Overall					Pts	GA
		W	D	L	F	A	W	D	L	F	A	W	D	L	F	A		
1 Derby County	42	16	4	1	43	16	10	7	4	22	16	26	11	5	65	32	63	2.03
2 Crystal Palace	42	14	4	3	45	24	8	8	5	25	23	22	12	8	70	47	56	1.49
3 Charlton Athletic	42	11	8	2	39	21	7	6	8	22	31	18	14	10	61	52	50	1.17
4 Middlesbrough	42	13	7	1	36	13	6	4	11	22	36	19	11	12	58	49	49	1.18
5 Cardiff City	42	13	3	5	38	19	7	4	10	29	35	20	7	15	67	54	47	1.24
6 Huddersfield Town	42	13	6	2	37	14	4	6	11	16	32	17	12	13	53	46	46	1.15
7 Birmingham City	42	13	3	5	52	24	5	5	11	21	35	18	8	16	73	59	44	1.24
8 Blackpool	42	9	8	4	33	20	5	7	9	18	21	14	15	13	51	41	43	1.24
9 Sheffield United	42	14	4	3	41	15	2	7	12	20	35	16	11	15	61	50	43	1.22
10 Millwall	42	10	5	6	33	23	7	4	10	24	26	17	9	16	57	49	43	1.16
11 Hull City	42	10	7	4	38	20	3	9	9	21	32	13	16	13	59	52	42	1.13
12 **Carlisle United**	42	10	5	6	25	17	6	5	10	21	32	16	10	16	46	49	42	0.94
13 Norwich City	42	7	6	8	24	25	8	4	9	29	31	15	10	17	53	56	40	0.95
14 Preston North End	42	8	8	5	23	19	4	7	10	15	25	12	15	15	38	44	39	0.86
15 Portsmouth	42	11	5	5	39	22	1	9	11	19	36	12	14	16	58	58	38	1.00
16 Bristol City	42	9	9	3	30	15	2	7	12	16	38	11	16	15	46	53	38	0.87
17 Bolton Wanderers	42	8	7	6	29	26	4	7	10	26	41	12	14	16	55	67	38	0.82
18 Aston Villa	42	10	8	3	22	11	2	6	13	15	37	12	14	16	37	48	38	0.77
19 Blackburn Rovers	42	9	6	6	30	24	4	5	12	22	39	13	11	18	52	63	37	0.83
20 Oxford United	42	8	5	8	21	23	4	4	13	13	32	12	9	21	34	55	33	0.62
21 Bury	42	8	4	9	35	33	3	4	14	16	47	11	8	23	51	80	30	0.64
22 Fulham	42	6	7	8	20	28	1	4	16	20	53	7	11	24	40	81	25	0.49

Bradford City in the McConnell Years:

Season 1969/70

Sat 09 Aug	Fulham (A)	0-0
Wed 13 Aug	Chesterfield (H) LgCR1	1-1
Sat 16 Aug	Torquay United (H)	2-1
Wed 20 Aug	Chesterfield (A) LgCR1R	1-0
Sat 23 Aug	Halifax Town (A)	0-0
Wed 27 Aug	Walsall (H)	3-0
Sat 30 Aug	Southport (H)	1-0
Wed 03 Sep	Sunderland (A) LgCR2	2-1
Sat 06 Sep	Mansfield Town (A)	1-2
Sat 13 Sep	Luton Town (H)	1-1
Mon 15 Sep	Orient (A)	1-2
Sat 20 Sep	Rochdale (A)	2-1
Wed 24 Sep	Southend United (H) LgCR3	2-1
Sat 27 Sep	Brighton & Hove Albion (H)	1-0
Wed 01 Oct	Reading (H)	4-0
Sat 04 Oct	Rotherham United (A)	3-2
Wed 08 Oct	Torquay United (A)	1-2
Sat 11 Oct	Barnsley (H)	1-1
Wed 15 Oct	West Bromwich Albion (A) LgCR4	0-4
Sat 18 Oct	Plymouth Argyle (H)	1-0
Sat 25 Oct	Shrewsbury Town (A)	0-1
Sat 01 Nov	Gillingham (H)	1-0
Sat 08 Nov	Bury (A)	2-0
Sat 15 Nov	Grimsby Town (H) FA1	2-1
Sat 22 Nov	Bristol Rovers (A)	1-1
Sat 29 Nov	Stockport County (H)	1-0
Mon 01 Dec	Barrow (A)	1-0
Sat 06 Dec	Lincoln City (H) FA2	3-0
Sat 13 Dec	Luton Town (A)	0-5
Fri 26 Dec	Halifax Town (H)	2-1
Sat 03 Jan	Tottenham Hotspur (H) FA3	2-2
Wed 07 Jan	Tottenham Hotspur (A) FA3R	0-5
Wed 14 Jan	Reading (A)	0-1
Sat 17 Jan	Brighton & Hove Albion (A)	1-2
Sat 24 Jan	Bournemouth & Boscombe Ath (H).	8-1
Sat 31 Jan	Rotherham United (H)	0-1
Wed 04 Feb	Rochdale (H)	0-3
Sat 07 Feb	Barnsley (A)	2-3
Sat 14 Feb	Fulham (H)	0-0
Sat 21 Feb	Shrewsbury Town (H)	2-2
Wed 25 Feb	Tranmere Rovers (H)	1-1
Sat 28 Feb	Plymouth Argyle (A)	1-0
Tue 03 Mar	Doncaster Rovers (A)	1-1

Sat 07 Mar	Bristol Rovers (H)	2-4
Sat 14 Mar	Stockport County (A)	2-0
Mon 16 Mar	Tranmere Rovers (A)	0-1
Sat 21 Mar	Doncaster Rovers (H)	3-0
Fri 27 Mar	Gillingham (A)	1-1
Sat 28 Mar	Bournemouth & Boscombe Ath (A)	0-0
Mon 30 Mar	Bury (H)	0-1
Sat 04 Apr	Walsall (A)	0-2
Wed 08 Apr	Barrow (H)	3-3
Wed 15 Apr	Orient (H)	0-1
Wed 22 Apr	Mansfield Town (H)	0-1
Fri 24 Apr	Southport (A)	0-1

Division 3 Final Standings 1969/70	Pld	Home					Away					Overall					Pts	GA
		W	D	L	F	A	W	D	L	F	A	W	D	L	F	A		
1 Orient	46	16	5	2	43	15	9	7	7	24	21	25	12	9	67	36	62	1.86
2 Luton Town	46	13	8	2	46	15	10	6	7	31	28	23	14	9	77	43	60	1.79
3 Bristol Rovers	46	15	5	3	51	26	5	11	7	29	33	20	16	10	80	59	56	1.36
4 Fulham	46	12	9	2	43	26	8	6	9	38	29	20	15	11	81	55	55	1.47
5 Brighton & Hove Albion	46	16	4	3	37	16	7	5	11	20	27	23	9	14	57	43	55	1.33
6 Mansfield Town	46	14	4	5	46	22	7	7	9	24	27	21	11	14	70	49	53	1.43
7 Barnsley	46	14	6	3	43	24	5	9	9	25	35	19	15	12	68	59	53	1.15
8 Reading	46	16	3	4	52	29	5	8	10	35	48	21	11	14	87	77	53	1.13
9 Rochdale	46	11	6	6	39	24	7	4	12	30	36	18	10	18	69	60	46	1.15
10 Bradford City	46	11	6	6	37	22	6	6	11	20	28	17	12	17	57	50	46	1.14
11 Doncaster Rovers	46	13	4	6	31	19	4	8	11	21	35	17	12	17	52	54	46	0.96
12 Walsall	46	11	4	8	33	31	6	8	9	21	36	17	12	17	54	67	46	0.81
13 Torquay United	46	9	9	5	36	22	5	8	10	26	37	14	17	15	62	59	45	1.05
14 Rotherham United	46	10	8	5	36	19	5	6	12	26	35	15	14	17	62	54	44	1.15
15 Shrewsbury Town	46	10	12	1	35	17	3	6	14	27	46	13	18	15	62	63	44	0.98
16 Tranmere Rovers	46	10	8	5	38	29	4	8	11	18	43	14	16	16	56	72	44	0.78
17 Plymouth Argyle	46	10	7	6	32	23	6	4	13	24	41	16	11	19	56	64	43	0.88
18 Halifax Town	46	10	9	4	31	25	4	6	13	16	38	14	15	17	47	63	43	0.75
19 Bury	46	13	4	6	47	29	2	7	14	28	51	15	11	20	75	80	41	0.94
20 Gillingham	46	7	6	10	28	33	6	7	10	24	31	13	13	20	52	64	39	0.81
21 Bournemouth & Bosc. Ath.	46	8	9	6	28	27	4	6	13	20	44	12	15	19	48	71	39	0.68
22 Southport	46	11	5	7	31	22	3	5	15	17	44	14	10	22	48	66	38	0.73
23 Barrow	46	7	9	7	28	27	1	5	17	18	54	8	14	24	46	81	30	0.57
24 Stockport County	46	4	7	12	17	30	2	4	17	10	41	6	11	29	27	71	23	0.38

Season 1970/71

Sat 15 Aug	Walsall (A)	2-1
Wed 19 Aug	Halifax Town (A) LgCR1	2-3
Sat 22 Aug	Barnsley (H)	1-0
Sat 29 Aug	Rochdale (A)	0-0
Wed 02 Sep	Fulham (A)	0-5
Sat 05 Sep	Shrewsbury Town (H)	1-0
Sat 12 Sep	Brighton & Hove Albion (A)	2-1
Sat 19 Sep	Plymouth Argyle (H)	0-1
Wed 23 Sep	Wrexham (H)	1-3
Sat 26 Sep	Chesterfield (A)	1-0
Wed 30 Sep	Reading (H)	0-1
Fri 02 Oct	Preston North End (H)	0-2
Sat 10 Oct	Swansea City (A)	0-2
Sat 17 Oct	Walsall (H)	0-0
Mon 19 Oct	Tranmere Rovers (A)	1-3
Sat 24 Oct	Torquay United (H)	2-0
Sat 31 Oct	Halifax Town (A)	2-1
Sat 07 Nov	Rotherham United (H)	1-1
Tue 10 Nov	Bristol Rovers (A)	2-4
Sat 14 Nov	Bury (A)	1-1
Fri 20 Nov	Mansfield Town (H)	1-1
Sat 21 Nov	Macclesfield Town (H) FA1	3-2
Sat 05 Dec	Aston Villa (A)	0-1
Sat 12 Dec	Lincoln City (A) FA2	2-2
Wed 16 Dec	Lincoln City (H) FA2R1	2-2
Sat 19 Dec	Barnsley (A)	0-2
Mon 21 Dec	Lincoln City (neutral venue) FA2R2	1-4
Sat 26 Dec	Doncaster Rovers (H)	3-0
Sat 09 Jan	Reading (A)	1-1
Tue 12 Jan	Gillingham (A)	1-2
Sat 16 Jan	Tranmere Rovers (H)	1-1
Sat 23 Jan	Port Vale (H)	1-1
Sat 30 Jan	Mansfield Town (A)	5-3
Sat 06 Feb	Aston Villa (H)	1-0
Fri 12 Feb	Port Vale (A)	0-0
Sat 20 Feb	Bristol Rovers (H)	1-1
Mon 22 Feb	Wrexham (A)	0-2
Sat 27 Feb	Halifax Town (H)	0-1
Sat 06 Mar	Torquay United (A)	1-1
Sat 13 Mar	Bury (H)	1-3
Wed 17 Mar	Gillingham (H)	0-1
Sat 20 Mar	Rotherham United (A)	1-1
Sat 27 Mar	Shrewsbury Town (A)	1-1
Sat 03 Apr	Rochdale (H)	3-0
Sat 10 Apr	Doncaster Rovers (A)	1-3

Mon 12 Apr	Brighton & Hove Albion (H)	2-3
Tue 13 Apr	Preston North End (A)	1-1
Sat 17 Apr	Swansea City (H)	0-2
Sat 24 Apr	Plymouth Argyle (A)	3-1
Wed 28 Apr	Fulham (H)	2-3
Sat 01 May	Chesterfield (H)	1-0

Division 3 Final Standings 1970/71	Pld	Home					Away					Overall					Pts	GA
		W	D	L	F	A	W	D	L	F	A	W	D	L	F	A		
1 Preston North End	46	15	8	0	42	16	7	9	7	21	23	22	17	7	63	39	61	1.62
2 Fulham	46	15	6	2	39	12	9	6	8	29	29	24	12	10	68	41	60	1.66
3 Halifax Town	46	16	2	5	46	22	6	10	7	28	33	22	12	12	74	55	56	1.35
4 Aston Villa	46	13	7	3	27	13	6	8	9	27	33	19	15	12	54	46	53	1.17
5 Chesterfield	46	13	8	2	45	12	4	9	10	21	26	17	17	12	66	38	51	1.74
6 Bristol Rovers	46	11	5	7	38	24	8	8	7	31	26	19	13	14	69	50	51	1.38
7 Mansfield Town	46	13	7	3	44	28	5	8	10	20	34	18	15	13	64	62	51	1.03
8 Rotherham United	46	12	10	1	38	19	5	6	12	26	41	17	16	13	64	60	50	1.07
9 Wrexham	46	12	8	3	43	25	6	5	12	29	40	18	13	15	72	65	49	1.11
10 Torquay United	46	12	6	5	37	26	7	5	11	17	31	19	11	16	54	57	49	0.95
11 Swansea City	46	11	5	7	41	25	4	11	8	18	31	15	16	15	59	56	46	1.05
12 Barnsley	46	12	6	5	30	19	5	5	13	19	33	17	11	18	49	52	45	0.94
13 Shrewsbury Town	46	11	6	6	37	28	5	7	11	21	34	16	13	17	58	62	45	0.94
14 Brighton & Hove Albion	46	8	10	5	28	20	6	6	11	22	27	14	16	16	50	47	44	1.06
15 Plymouth Argyle	46	6	12	5	39	33	6	7	10	24	30	12	19	15	63	63	43	1.00
16 Rochdale	46	8	8	7	29	26	6	7	10	32	42	14	15	17	61	68	43	0.90
17 Port Vale	46	11	6	6	29	18	4	6	13	23	41	15	12	19	52	59	42	0.88
18 Tranmere Rovers	46	8	11	4	27	18	2	11	10	18	37	10	22	14	45	55	42	0.82
19 Bradford City	46	7	6	10	23	25	6	8	9	26	37	13	14	19	49	62	40	0.79
20 Walsall	46	10	1	12	30	27	4	10	9	21	30	14	11	21	51	57	39	0.89
21 Reading	46	10	7	6	32	33	4	4	15	16	52	14	11	21	48	85	39	0.56
22 Bury	46	7	9	7	30	23	5	4	14	22	37	12	13	21	52	60	37	0.87
23 Doncaster Rovers	46	8	5	10	28	27	5	4	14	17	39	13	9	24	45	66	35	0.68
24 Gillingham	46	6	9	8	22	29	4	4	15	20	38	10	13	23	42	67	33	0.63

They picked the BEST EVER team
(Evening News 1965)

Back in the mid-60's the readers of the local paper were handed the unenviable task of picking the best ever Carlisle United starting eleven from the pool of literally hundreds of heroes who had turned out in a blue shirt since the club had joined the Football League back in August 1928.

Just under 1000 fans replied, and their votes were cast as follows:

Keepers

Thompson	365
Jones	235
Mclaren	150
Dean	136

Right Backs

Neil	367
Hutton	364
McIntosh	302
Gallagher	111

Right Halves

McConnell	422
Kinloch	213
Bradley	155
Johnston	77

Centre Halves

Twentyman	460
Passmoor	138
Taylor	176
Waters	107

Left Halves

Harland	572
Stokoe	110
Whiteman	107
Thompson	76

Outside Rights

Hogan	846
Blain	31

Inside Rights

Broadis	846
Turner	36

Centre Forwards

McIlmoyle	686
Ackerman	147
Lindsay	42

Inside Lefts

Dougal	435
Davies	219
Dick	95
Carlin	71

Outside Lefts

Simpson	536
Taylor	149
McCue	101

Mum at the Cotton Mill ahead
of a shift in the chip shop

The young brothers
looking very smart

Dad and me, with the Margaret Street
'football pitch' in the background

The Mayor of Stockport
meets the Brigadoons

Barry as our proud mascot

Water all-round for the Kerbside Cup winners

The Stockport U15 Boys Team

Leeds United Juniors 1 - 0 Northern Intermediate Select
- at Roker Park, 7 Dec 1955 (I was captain)

I am third from the right, middle row, with John Reynolds
immediately to my right

The club blazer in all its glory   Mary not long after we met

National Service
over and back to
work with Gerry
Francis, Don
Revie, Terry
Caldwell, Freddie
Goodwin, et al

The big day at St Wilfreds Church

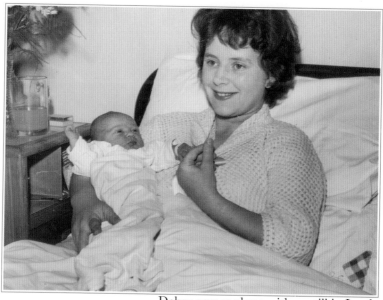

Debra comes along with us still in Leeds

A stunned Leeds dressing room learns that
Don Revie has taken over

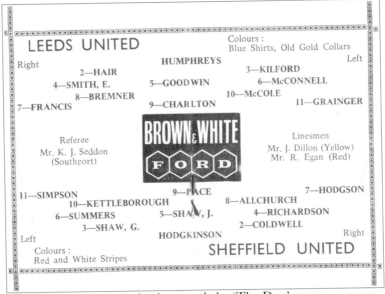

One of the first team selections made by 'The Don'

Not long before I left Elland Road for Cumbria

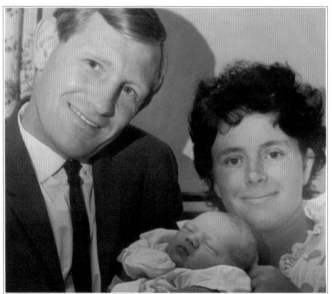

Cath and James join the family over in Carlisle

The basketball boots that caused so many
problems with Dick Young

Letting one fly at Workington on a cold December day

With the keeper beaten, Dick Young said, 'Nice One Skip'